Offering Ourselves:

A Lenten Journey
with
Charlotte Mason

by

Anne E. White

CONTENTS

Introduction

> Life batters and shapes us in all sorts of ways before it's done, but those original selves which we were born with and which I believe we continue in some measure to be no matter what are selves which still echo with the holiness of their origin. (Frederick Buechner, *Telling Secrets*)

> What a reason have we here for doing whatever in us lies towards giving every person in the world the chance of being all that he came into the world provided and intended to be! (*Ourselves Book I*, pp. 79-80)

This book is both a sequel and a prequel. A few years ago I wrote a series of Advent-themed blog posts which drew on Charlotte Mason's *Ourselves, Book II*, and they became the book *Honest, Simple Souls*. This book, similarly, follows the chapters of *Book I*, with the intention that it be read through the forty days of Lent, from Ash Wednesday to Holy Saturday. (Readings for Sundays are also included, although Sundays are designated as "Little Easters.")

What is *Ourselves* about?

Charlotte called *Ourselves* "…an ordered presentation of the possibilities that lie in human nature, and of the risks that attend these…an appeal to the young to make the most of themselves, because of the vast possibilities that are in them and of the law of God which constrains them." (Preface to *Ourselves*)

Isn't it meant as a children's book?

Sort of.

Ourselves is known as the book that Charlotte Mason wrote for students, and when you look at some of the language she uses, you might get the impression that she was writing for, maybe, children aged eight to ten. For example, in Chapter I, on Hunger: "Never think of your meals tills they come, and, while you are eating, talk and think of something more amusing than your food. As for nice things, of course we all want nice things now and then; but let us eat what is given to us of the chocolate or fruit at table, and not think any more about it." But then there's Chapter IV, on Chastity, and when I was ten I wouldn't have understood even the word, much less what she was talking about.

So for whom did she actually write the book, and how did she intend it to be used? The Preface says, "The teaching in *Book I* is designed for boys and girls under sixteen," and "That in *Book II* should, perhaps, appeal to young people of any age"; also that "In the hands of the teachers of elementary schools, the book should give some help in the formation of character." In the Parents' Union School programmes, *Book I* wasn't scheduled until what we would call middle school, for students aged twelve to fifteen, and *Book II* was read in the final years of high school. Also, all the students would have been reading the same parts of the book at the same time; so there might have been twelve-year-olds reading the end of *Book I*, about Vocation, and others not getting to the part about chocolate and fruit until they were fifteen.

However, that doesn't mean that *Ourselves* can't be used with slightly younger children, or with mixed years; or that it doesn't have applications for people over those ages, for instance an adult study group; or even that it has to be read chapter by chapter.

> I think that in teaching children mothers should
> make their own of so much as they wish to give of
> such teaching, and speak it, a little at a time,
> perhaps by way of Sunday talks. This would help to
> impress children with the thought that our relations
> with God embrace the whole of our lives.
> (*Ourselves*, Introduction)

Three Purposes for this Study

Many reading this book will be at least somewhat familiar with Charlotte Mason's philosophy of education. It is useful to look at how what Charlotte presents here lines up with her list of educational principles, and her other ideas such as the importance of habit; and we will also want to see if the things she says about education and the training of children are practical and Scriptural. Second, we may find things that have practical value for our own lives, maybe something as simple as enjoying plain water, or a more complex idea such as justice in our thought life.

A third hope is that it may inspire those who teach their own children, or students in a school classroom, or in another setting such as a Sunday school; who wish to communicate the important ideas of *Ourselves*, but who for whatever reason cannot read it to them directly.

The Principles and the Kingdom

Charlotte Mason's principles are not simply an educational (i.e. academic) creed; they are life lessons. *Ourselves* is the book in which she brings her phrase "moral and intellectual self-management" (Principle 16) to life. It examines all of the final principles on the list, including #17, the Way of the Will; #18, the Way of Reason; and the last two:

> 19. Therefore, children should be taught, as they become mature enough to understand such teaching, that the chief responsibility which rests on them *as persons* is the acceptance or rejection of ideas. To help them in this choice we give them principles of conduct, and a wide range of the knowledge fitted to them. These principles should save children from some of the loose thinking and heedless action which cause most of us to live at a lower level than we need.

> 20. We allow no separation to grow up between the intellectual and 'spiritual' life of children, but teach them that the Divine Spirit has constant access to their spirits, and is their Continual Helper in all the interests, duties and joys of life.

Ourselves uses an allegorical framework borrowed from John Bunyan's *The Holy War*. Each of us exists as a kingdom called "Mansoul," full of beauty, courage, and other undiscovered potential; but we have much to learn about its government, such as the struggles for power between various "lords" and their dreams and desires.

> This inner self is, as we have said, like a vast
> country much of which is not yet explored, or like a
> great house, built as a maze, in which you cannot
> find your way about. (p. 33)

But what is the book *about*? If we drop the lords and the houses of this and that, what remains? As we've just read: five very packed statements about the "persons" who are all of our selves.

> ...to be born a human being is like coming into a
> very great estate; so much in the way of goodness,
> greatness, heroism, wisdom, and knowledge, is
> possible to us all. (p. 9)

Now, any good thing can become a bad thing if it is out of balance; any desire, though natural and healthy in itself, can enslave us. Mansoul's daily issues and decisions must be brought to the attention of the Will, who acts as "Prime Minister"; but Will himself also serves Christ, the King of the land, and (as Principle 20 says), has constant access to the Holy Spirit.

What is the "chief responsibility which rests on us *as persons*?" "The acceptance or rejection of ideas," says Principle 19. If "loose thinking and heedless action...causes most of us to live at a lower level than we need," then we need more focused thinking and deliberate action. We need the discipline of a well-ordered inner "government" to give us a better life: better not in a self-focused or material sense, but more fit and ready to serve in the Kingdom of God. Does that put too much focus on the Self? Charlotte says no:

> There are so many interesting things in the world to
> discuss that [we may think] it is a waste of time to
> talk about *ourselves*. All the same, it is well to be up
> to the ways of those tiresome selves, and that is why
> you are invited to read these chapters. (pp. 129-130)

What is the connection between *Ourselves* and the seasons of the church year?

> To journey for the sake of saving our own lives is
> little by little to cease to live in any sense that really
> matters, even to ourselves, because it is only by
> journeying for the world's sake–even when the

world bores and sickens and scares you half to
death–that little by little we start to come alive.
(Frederick Buechner, *The Sacred Journey*)

Ourselves begins by asking us to consider the landscape around us, and then our physical needs and appetites (not a bad theme during a traditional time of fasting); but she quickly moves on to what goes on inside our deepest thoughts and imaginings, and then takes up two major threads of Love and Justice. Do we begin to see some connections?

Kevin P. Emmert, an online editor for *Christianity Today*, wrote an article called "A Lent That's Not For Your Spiritual Improvement." He criticizes the idea that giving up something during Lent is done primarily for our own spiritual strength, any more than, say, a God-inspired course of weightlifting is an end in itself. Yes, we "look within ourselves, to examine our hearts and surrender them to Christ." But we also "look to others, to see how we might serve and lay down our lives for others as Christ has done for us." And, ultimately, "Lent teaches us to look to Christ as our sole redeemer and source of strength."

This is, I think, where the journeys run in parallel lines.

Along the Way

In *Honest, Simple Souls*, each entry was followed by a thought or practical suggestion, called "In the spirit of the season." I had planned to do the same in this book, to suggest Lent-season things that people could do: take nature walks, read poetry, listen to music that stirred their spirits. Share food with others. Send cards or write notes. Pray for each other. All those things that we might be doing anyway.

However, the more I worked on this, the less useful it seemed to randomly suggest things to listen to or books to read. This journey is about *all our selves*, and I do not want to intrude with my seemingly bright ideas. Maybe it's a happy day and you want to do something fun. Maybe it's a tear-filled one, or one where the most you can do is read and maybe pray.

Therefore, many of the **Along the Way** sections are intentionally left blank for your own notes and thoughts. (If you are reading a digital version, you may want to keep a notebook in some other form.)

A Few Notes

All quotations giving only page numbers are from *Ourselves,* and they are all from *Book I* unless otherwise stated.

All Scripture quotes are from the King James Version.

The material about William Morris (**Sunday Interval #5**) is from a talk given at the 2022 L'HaRMaS, a Charlotte Mason retreat held in Kingsville, Ontario.

"I give you yourselves"

The Lion opened his mouth, but no sound came from it; he was breathing out, a long, warm breath; it seemed to sway all the beasts as the wind sways a line of trees…and every drop of blood tingled in the children's bodies, and the deepest, wildest voice they had ever heard was saying: "Narnia, Narnia, Narnia, awake. Love. Think. Speak. Be walking trees. Be talking beasts. Be divine waters…"

"Creatures, I give you yourselves," said the strong, happy voice of Aslan. "I give to you forever this land of Narnia. I give you the woods, the fruits, the rivers. I give you the stars and I give you myself…"

"And now," said Aslan, "Narnia is established. We must next take thought for keeping it safe. I will call some of you to my council. Come hither to me, you the chief Dwarf, and you the River-god, and you Oak and the He-Owl, and both the Ravens and the Bull-Elephant. We must talk together. For though the world is not five hours old an evil has already entered it."

(C.S. Lewis, *The Magician's Nephew*)

Day 1: The Journey Begins on Ash Wednesday

"The rue is a bitter-leafed herb. Rue is repentance.
Rue is compassion. Old Don Quixote was the knight
of the rueful countenance, and he was a pilgrim,
poor old chap." (Elizabeth Goudge, *Pilgrim's Inn*)

Charlotte is clear on her purpose for this book, no matter at what age we read it. She wants each of us to discover what we are, "the ground-plan of human nature," the "common possession"; which if you think about it, is a pretty radical thought for the intended age group, because the early teens are a time when we both want to fit in with other people and see our own selves as unique.

...when we learn to think of ourselves as one of the
rest, with just the same rights as other people and
no more, to whom others owe just such duties as we
owe to them and no more, we shall, as it were, get
our lives in focus and see things as they are.
(*Ourselves* p. 139)

And the second is like, namely this, Thou shalt love
thy neighbour as thyself. There is none other
commandment greater than these. (Mark 12:31)

But it is not only our "wonderful self" that we have to deal with, but our "awful self." In her introduction to the book, Charlotte describes how children and teenagers get a "sense of the worthlessness of this poor, pushing, all too prominent self." No matter what the age, the problem is self itself. In Elizabeth Goudge's novel *Pilgrim's Inn*, one of the adult characters is called to let go of a relationship she has selfishly held onto, and this will free not only the others caught in its mess, but herself as well.

Subtly, with no clear word spoken, yet he had made
her face it. He demanded of her the ultimate denial,
without reservation, and correlated with that the
ultimate giving, without reservation. He asked of

her the single mind, the herb of grace.

"The single mind," the "bitter-leafed herb" of pulling in, cutting back, narrowing—fasting—so that we can give ourselves more fully to the rightful recipients of our love.

Scriptures to Ponder

> Is not this the fast that I have chosen? to loose the
> bands of wickedness, to undo the heavy burdens,
> and to let the oppressed go free, and that ye break
> every yoke? (Isaiah 58:6)

Along the Way

Decluttering expert Dana K. White has written about how she used to have multiple wooden spoons in her kitchen, most found cheaply at yard sales. Having so many was an advantage when she did not always have clean dishes, as there was always another one to pull out. However, when she established a habit of daily dish-washing, she found not only that she didn't need so many spoons, but that she was now able to use her best and favourite one whenever she liked.

In this season when many Christians fast or give up something, consider an alternative. If you have multiple objects or choices in some area of your life: choose just one among them to wear, listen to, eat, drink, read, or otherwise use for the next forty days. Keep whatever it is clean and available, and perhaps put the other choices away so that you are not tempted to wear or eat something else. Pull back on something so that you can practice giving yourself fully.

Day 2: The Country Through Which We Travel

> ...a curious thing is, that no map has been made of
> the country, because a great deal of it is unexplored,
> and men have not discovered its boundaries...there
> are everywhere reaches which no man has seen,

regions of country which may be rich and beautiful.
(p. 4)

...she realized that he had got her and got
everything. His love held and illumined every
human being for whom she was concerned, and
whom she served with the profound compassion
which was their need and right, held the Cathedral,
the city, every flower and leaf and creature, giving it
reality and beauty. (Elizabeth Goudge, *The Dean's
Watch*)

Charlotte's description of the "Ourselves" country is pastoral; not
completely idyllic (as she cautions in the next chapter), but at least full
of "fertile soil," with all kinds of cultivated crops and some wild things
too. Even the wilderness places "only wait for good and industrious
hands to reclaim them and make them as fertile as the rest of the
country." There are workplaces such as factories; there seems to be a
solid mining industry, with much that's buried being unearthed. But
there are also "palaces of delight," places to hear music, see art, and
read "every book of delight that ever was written." And there are
churches, which represent the deepest places of our spiritual life.

But imagining each person as a whole country or kingdom, perhaps
a Narnia (though not a Utopia), can be overwhelming and sometimes
confusing. We may have to mentally scale back, and begin by thinking
of a walk through something like the town described by Goudge: "the
Cathedral, the city, every flower and leaf and creature." How well do
we know our own "City? "How much time have we spent enjoying its
parks and libraries? Are we aware of its main businesses and resources?
Have we talked with the town council about plans for the rose festival
and the budget for road repairs? Do we find ourselves somewhat
reluctant and overawed (like one of Goudge's characters) to set foot in
the Cathedral?

It is true that humans are fallen beings, along with the rest of
Creation, and it is not my theological place to debate how far the falling
was. However, each of us is, unequivocally, made in God's image,
inheriting characteristics such as the ability to imagine, create, and love.
We need to begin by acknowledging that, and by thanking Him for it,
even if the Person-City limits seem enough for us to begin with. Then
we'll set off to explore the fields, the mountains, and the waterfalls,

and even the Place Beyond.

"What's the Place Beyond?" asked Sally.

"What the other places aren't," said Jerry...

(Elizabeth Goudge, *Pilgrim's Inn*)

Scriptures to Ponder

...for the LORD seeth not as man seeth; for man
looketh on the outward appearance, but the
LORD looketh on the heart. (1 Sam. 16:7)

Along the Way

Each Person-Kingdom was created to be a land of beauty: not just an idyll for lotus-eaters, but a productive and healthy place where government, business, leisure, learning, and worship all function together to serve the King. Take a mental walk around your "place," and describe it in any format you choose (a map, a drawing, a verbal description). If you feel like the river is polluted, the buildings are falling apart and the government officials are all trying to impeach each other, does it at least have a good climate? Our personal kingdoms all have their share of crumbling castles, dark forests, and rocky inlets, and these will be described over the next two readings. For now, though, try to focus on the positive features of the Person-City.

Day 3: Don't Get Swamped

Part One

We are now shown the less-beautiful side of our Mansoul: the thorns, thistles, and sloughs, the floods and fires, the damage caused by wars, accidents, or neglect. All things, if not taken care of, tend to break down and stop running. Even from our place in the city, we see graffiti, broken water mains, and potholes.

Fruit drops from the trees and rots because no one
cares to pick it up...The librarians let their books be
buried in dust and devoured by insects, and neglect

their duty of gathering more. (pp. 5-6)

When we acknowledge the broken parts and the ugly spots in our Mansoul (or Self-Land or Person-City), we may ask, first off, whose fault it is that they are in such bad shape. Then we ask how we can correct the weak links in the government of our lives. Is the problem that our "elected officials" are not doing enough, or that they're taking on too much or acting where they shouldn't?

> If each would attend to his own business and
> nothing else, all would go well; but there is a great
> deal of rivalry in the government, and every
> member tries to make the Prime Minister believe
> that the happiness of Mansoul depends upon him. If
> any one of these gets things altogether into his
> hands, all is in disorder. (p. 11)

Second, can the existing damage be repaired, and how? Third, how can we prevent such damage, keep dams from bursting and books from being chewed? If we are Christians, we may ask whether all the repairs and restoration are completed at once, through God's saving grace; or whether, like any land under the rule of a new king, old broken walls (and damaged books) may take time to be repaired, and new problems may occur as well. Is the issue one of deliverance from sin through the power of the Holy Spirit? Or are we talking about something for which we have control and responsibility?

> Every human being, child or man, is a Kingdom of
> Mansoul; and to be born a human being is like
> coming into a very great estate; so much in the way
> of goodness, greatness, heroism, wisdom, and
> knowledge, is possible to us all. (p. 9)

Our "city council" has authority to make bylaws, issue parking tickets, plant flower beds, and keep the streets safe; and they must do the jobs they've been given. For Charlotte, it wasn't an either/or question, but both at once: the monarch was to be served and obeyed, and a loyal government was to do all it could to keep the kingdom in order.

Scriptures to Ponder

He also that received seed among the thorns is he

that heareth the word; and the care of this world,
and the deceitfulness of riches, choke the word, and
he becometh unfruitful.

But he that received seed into the good ground is he
that heareth the word, and understandeth it; which
also beareth fruit, and bringeth forth, some an
hundredfold, some sixty, some thirty.

(Matthew 13:22-23)

Along the Way

If you created a description of your Person-Place's assets, you may
want to balance that out today by listing some of its less attractive
features. Which issues have clear enough solutions to be dealt with by
the town council? Are there dust-covered library books? Is there
garbage that needs to be picked up, flowers that need to be tended?
And are there deeper concerns that need to go straight to the King?

Day 4: Through the Mists

Out of the night that covers me
Black as the pit from pole to pole,
I thank whatever gods may be
For my unconquerable soul.

(William Ernest Henley, "Invictus")

As an interesting and somewhat controversial end point to her list of
dangers, Charlotte describes what is, more or less, depression:
"chilling, soaking mists, dense and black; not a ray of the sun can
penetrate these mists, no light, no warmth; there is no seeing of one's
way..." One senses that Charlotte has walked through some of these
mists herself. She promises to talk about a remedy later in the story,
but for now it is enough to say that they are a recognized
environmental hazard in Mansoul. Some lands are more prone to mists
than others, but it seems important to know that none are totally
immune; that most have had or will have some experience of darkness

that blots out the sun.

John Bunyan wrote about similar experiences in *The Pilgrim's Progress*, showing that they can be part of even a Christian's journey. Bunyan's hero Christian first falls into a muddy swamp, and splashes around hopelessly until he is rescued by an angel named Help. Later on, he finds himself imprisoned in Doubting Castle by Giant Despair, and is freed only when he uses the Key of Promise. He also travels through dark valleys and fights with terrifying monsters.

Do all these problems and perils and pains make the Self-land a bad place to live in, or to travel through? No, although our journey may not be easy. Like Christian, we are blessed with companions named Faith(ful) and Hope(ful); and there is another Friend who has promised not to forsake us. Remember the final principle?

> 20. We allow no separation to grow up between the intellectual and 'spiritual' life of children, but teach them that the Divine Spirit has constant access to their spirits, and is their Continual Helper in all the interests, duties and joys of life.

Scriptures to Ponder

> He shall call upon me, and I will answer him: I will be with him in trouble; I will deliver him, and honour him. With long life will I satisfy him, And shew him my salvation. (Psalm 91:15–16)

Along the Way

In Jan Karon's novel *In This Mountain*, Father Tim's post-accident depression is eased but not ended by the well-meaning attempts of those around him; even Uncle Billy's jokes don't quite cut it. Finally he preaches a sermon which includes these words:

> I admit to you that although I often thank God for my blessings, even the smallest, I haven't thanked him for my affliction. I've been too busy begging Him to lead me out of the valley and onto the mountain top. After all, I have work to do, I have things to accomplish...

Which parts of your Mansoul (or Self-Kingdom) are the most prone to falling rocks or dense fog? Are there places you should post warning signs (maybe on sticky notes on the bathroom mirror)? What would you write on them? (One suggestion from Father Tim's sermon: SLOW.)

Sunday Interlude #1

...when you look with dread upon the winter weeks
that lie before you, have you ever dreamed—in
office or kitchen or school—of leaving winter
behind, of meeting spring under far-southern skies,
of following its triumphal pilgrimage up the map
with flowers all the way, with singing birds and soft
air, green grass and trees new-clothed, of coming
north with the spring? That is a dream of the
winter-weary...My wife and I dreamed of knowing
something of all phases, of reading all possible
chapters, of seeing, firsthand, the long northward
flow of the season. (Edwin Way Teale, *North with
the Spring*)

Since we are trying to view *Ourselves* less as a class in civics and more as a Lenten pilgrimage, let's imagine that we plan for our physical needs on the journey. What will we eat and drink? Where will we rest? How will we keep ourselves clean while we travel? We will look at these things during this week's readings.

But we also turn our attention to the things we might see along the way. What do we know about them already? What makes us curious, or creates an emotional reaction? In *The Educated Imagination*, Northrop Frye asks his readers to imagine themselves on a desert island, simply observing what is around them. Frye says,

...looking at the world, as something set over
against you, splits your mind in two. You have an
intellect that feels curious about it and wants to
study it, and you have feelings or emotions that see
it as beautiful or austere or terrible...This is the
speculative or contemplative position of the mind,
the position in which the arts and sciences begin...

Charlotte says that we not only observe, reason, and imagine about the things we see around us, but that they also bring out our natural desires for things such as power, wealth, knowledge, and even the company and the approval of others. Which brings us to the characters living in the realms of the "heart": Love, Justice, and all their colleagues and underlings, friends and enemies. And finally to what we may call the Cathedral...or the Temple...the place where we explore the deepest reasons for our being.

> Beyond and above all these is the King; for you
> remember that Mansoul is a Kingdom. (p. 10)

Scriptures to Ponder

> When I consider thy heavens, the work of thy
> fingers, the moon and the stars, which thou hast
> ordained; What is man, that thou art mindful of
> him? and the son of man, that thou visitest him?
>
> (Psalm 8: 3-4)

Along the Way

What are you looking forward to most on this journey?

Day 5: The Picnic Basket

As in *The Pilgrim's Progress*, the story of *Ourselves* includes a number of allegorically-named characters. In Bunyan's story we have Talkative, Faithful, Hate-Good; in Mason we have Esquire Hunger, "Truth, the Handmaid of Justice," and the Chief Explorer Imagination. One difference, though, is that Bunyan's characters generally represent either good or evil, virtue or sin. The characters in this Mansoul usually have "possibilities for good or for evil." Much like people.

So we begin with Hunger, one of the appetites in the House of Body. Some of Charlotte's maxims about Hunger (and, later, Taste) may not sit well today with people who have food and body-image triggers. A few of them ("Never think of your meals till they come, and, while you are eating, talk and think of something more amusing than your food") may seem downright mysterious to those from cultures where talking and thinking about food is very important!

> But people who pamper Taste make themselves his
> servants. They say they do not like porridge; they do
> not like mutton, potatoes, eggs. They want things
> with strong flavours to please their Taste; the older
> they grow the more difficult it will be to gratify
> them... (pp. 24-25)

> One should eat to live, not live to eat. (Variously
> attributed to Socrates, Molière, and Jack LaLanne)

However, if we can get over those issues, there are two points we should unpack. First, that physical appetites, like other needs and desires, are natural and good. Feasting can be as important as fasting! Without a good appetite for meals, we would end up like the Slow-Eater-Tiny-Bite-Taker in *Mrs. Piggle-Wiggle*. Or the boy in *Struwwelpeter* who wasted away because he wouldn't eat his soup.

And second, that decisions involving Hunger are decided first by Habit, perhaps also by Reason, but finally by Will; so they offer a simple way to begin, and a model for more complex choices.

> Gluttony begins with the little boy and goes with
> him all through life, only that, instead of caring for
> chocolate creams when he is a man, he cares for
> great dinners two hours long. (p. 13)

Do we "eat in due season, for strength, and not for drunkenness" (Ecclesiastes 10:17)? Are we able to say yes to what is good and enough for us, and no to the rest? Might we (or our children) someday be in circumstances where we'll be glad of the ability to simply eat whatever there is and give thanks?

> "I'm trying to catch a few eels to make an eel stew
> for our dinner," said Puddleglum. "Though I
> shouldn't wonder if I didn't get any. And you won't
> like them much if I do..."

> When the meal came it was delicious and the
> children had two large helpings each. At first the
> Marsh-wiggle wouldn't believe that they really liked
> it, and when they had eaten so much that he had to

believe them, he fell back on saying that it would
probably disagree with them horribly.

(C.S. Lewis, *The Silver Chair*)

Charlotte Mason lived most of her life in rooms at the college in
Ambleside, and ate what was cooked and served by others. Many of us
have different food responsibilities than she did: planning, shopping,
cooking, cleaning up, trying to cope with busy schedules. Many parents
are rightly concerned about sourcing healthy food; and that effort is
doubled if someone needs a special diet. But in our concern for the
right things we can still find ourselves making too much of what we
eat. Edith Schaeffer wrote about a mealtime situation that had caused
friction in her daughter's family. Her son-in-law often got delayed in
coming home for lunch, and that meant both that the food got cold
and that he had little time to see his children. This situation seemed to
worry his wife much more than it did him, but one day she prayed
about the whole thing and came to one conclusion: stop fussing. When
she decided to let lunch be about the people, and the time they did
have to be together, things began to go much more smoothly.

In your own situation, would planning regular dinner menus help,
so that "what we feel like eating tonight" doesn't take charge? Having
fewer foods to choose from at a meal, or keeping desserts for
weekends or special times? If life has had too much pizza in it lately,
rekindling an appetite for simple, fresh foods? Or even, if you have
(Martha-like) found yourself spending too much time in the
kitchen…ordering some takeout, without guilt?

There is a time to read cookbooks…and a time to close them.

Scriptures to Ponder

> But he answered and said, It is written, Man shall
> not live by bread alone, but by every word that
> proceedeth out of the mouth of God. (Matthew 4:4)

> Whether therefore ye eat, or drink, or whatsoever ye
> do, do all to the glory of God. (1 Cor. 10:31)

Along the Way

What are some ways that you can employ Hunger as a good servant, without giving him more than his proper place?

Day 6: A Taste for Cold Water

> All little children like water, but bigger boys and
> girls sometimes like various things, such as lemon
> juice, in their water to give it a flavour. Though
> there is no harm in this, it is rather a pity, because
> they lose their taste for water itself. (pp. 15-16)

Charlotte makes two useful points in her chapter on thirst. First, that the simplest form of something may often be the best, if we have not spoiled our taste for it by insisting on variations and additions.

Second, that addictions, of any kind, hurt us and those around us, by taking up our "time, health, and strength." They promise us happiness by means that do not last long or fully satisfy. Even if we are not prone to a particular temptation, we may feel called to abstain from it simply as an example to others.

> Christian simplicity is...a call given to every
> Christian. The witness to simplicity is profoundly
> rooted in the biblical tradition, and most perfectly
> exemplified in the life of Jesus Christ. (Richard J.
> Foster, *Freedom of Simplicity*)

Scriptures to Ponder

> And take heed to yourselves, lest at any time your
> hearts be overcharged with surfeiting, and
> drunkenness, and cares of this life, and so that day
> come upon you unawares. (Luke 21:34)

Along the Way

How might a taste for plain water symbolize what Richard Foster calls the "freedom of simplicity?"

Day 7: A Rest Under the Trees

Charlotte says that "Restlessness makes the Body Strong." In other words, human bodies are wired to work, and move, and to use whatever physical strength we have to "walk far and to hit true and to do every service that the Prime Minister may require." Then we get hungry and want fuel, and get tired and want to rest: that's the natural way of things. It is only when we try to work–or not work–against those needs that we get ourselves into trouble.

Overdoing it

Remember the reference to the rue plant in Elizabeth Goudge's *Pilgrim's Inn*? Two of her characters discuss its special properties here:

> "...Astringent—that means contraction. Bitter to the taste. Repentant. Compassionate...I've got it...Single-mindedness."

> "But I've always thought of single-mindedness as a sort of concentration," said Sally.

> "Yes. Contraction. Everything gathered in for the giving of yourself. The whole of you. Nothing kept back."

Charlotte is all about what some people call mindfulness: *being* whenever and wherever you are, doing what you are supposed to be doing. Reading, practicing, chopping firewood, listening to a customer's complaint, playing with your children, sailing a boat, balancing an account, watching ants, planning a battle, praying. And resting fully in between. Why does this matter?

> [Letting your mind wander or trying to do too many things at once] is a very unfortunate state to get into, because it is only by going on doing one thing steadily that we learn to do it well, whether it be cricket or algebra; so it is well to be on the watch for the moment when Restlessness, the good servant, turns into Restlessness, the unquiet Daemon who drives us about from post to pillar, and will not give

us firm standing ground anywhere in life. (p. 19)

Firm ground is what we want: the very opposite of the muddy swamp.

Underdoing it

>...if your friends call you idle about play or
>work...pull yourself together without loss of time,
>for be sure the Daemon, Sloth, is upon you... (p. 20)

Sloth "can't bear games," Charlotte says; "does not want to make boats
or whistles, or collect stamps"; and, more importantly, "never does
anything for anybody...because he will not take the trouble." If we
repeatedly turn down our friends'...or our children's...requests for a
walk, a game, a special meal, small things that show them we care, then
they will be reluctant to ask when they need more serious help. Taking
the trouble benefits them, but it is also good for us.

And now it's time to pick up the food basket, strap on a backpack,
and leave our comfortable park benches behind. Adventure awaits.

>"Take the Adventure, heed the call, now ere the
>irrevocable moment passes! 'Tis but a banging of
>the door behind you, a blithesome step forward, and
>you are out of the old life into the new!" (Kenneth
>Grahame, *The Wind in the Willows*)

Scriptures to Ponder

>The Son of man came eating and drinking, and they
>say, Behold a man gluttonous, and a winebibber, a
>friend of publicans and sinners. (Matt. 11:18-19)

Along the Way

To do something with full energy and attention, we need focus only
on that one thing, not be halfway somewhere else. Sometimes that
means working alone, but sometimes (surprisingly) it can be better to
share an activity with someone else, so that you both keep your minds
on the task. This is, apparently, why Charlotte's student teachers went
out in pairs for their nature walks (noted in *The Story of Charlotte Mason*,
by Essex Cholmondeley). Whatever you need to do today, find a way

to do only that thing, alone or in company.

Day 8: "Thou, God, seest me"

"Because of Whose I Am" is a song by Reba Rambo and Dony McGuire that was recorded by various Christian singers of the 1980's. Part of it goes like this:

> His blood is flowing through my veins
> I'm adopted by the King
> It's because of whose
> Not because of what I am
> Not because of what I am
> Because of whose I am

In her chapter "Chastity," Charlotte speaks briefly and not too explicitly about physical purity. As she is supposedly writing to children, her message is that sexual urges are an important and natural appetite, but that too much interest in or knowledge about such matters would not be necessary or good for them. Whether we fully agree with her views or not, we need to consider this part of life as one more way in which we care for our physical bodies (and those of our children) and commit them to the service of God.

> The opposite virtue is called Purity, and Christ has
> said, "Blessed are the pure in heart, for they shall
> see God." That does not mean, I think, 'shall see
> God' when they die, but 'shall see' Him with the eye
> of their soul, about them and beside them, and shall
> know, whenever temptation comes through this
> Appetite— 'Thou, God, seest me.' (p. 22)

"God seest me" applies as much to adults as to children, and to all the other appetites as well: we need purity because of whose we are, who created us, and who bought us with a price (1 Cor. 6:20).

Scriptures to Ponder

> For where your treasure is, there will your heart be
> also. (Matt. 6:21)

Along the Way

As noted in the Introduction, some of the "Along the Way" sections are intentionally left blank. Please use them as your own "rest stops."

Day 9: A Motto for the Journey

The Fairy-Land of Science is a book that was used for many years in the Parents' Union School. It covers topics such as light, the atmosphere, the water cycle, the formation of crystals, magnets, snowflakes, ice and other precipitation, glaciers, how rivers and other bodies of water alter the land, soundwaves, how ears work, sounds in nature, the life of a primrose, where coal comes from, and what bees do.

Besides the obvious "light" and "soundwaves," what does all that have to do with our senses, and the role they play in Charlotte's analogy of the soul? Each science topic forces us to pay greater attention to the things around us, especially to the information we receive through the senses. We see the structure of crystals and beehives; we hear the river running and the insects humming; we touch the earth and handle the magnets. Nothing is just "there"; everything has a purpose. Frederick Buechner describes that sense of wonder in this way:

> The child in us lives in a world where nothing is too
> familiar or unpromising to open up into the world
> where a path unwinds before our feet into a deep
> wood, and when that happens, neither the world we
> live in nor the world that lives in us can ever
> entirely be home again... (*Telling the Truth*)

Buechner puts it more directly in another book:

> ...touch, taste, smell your way to the holy and
> hidden heart of [life] because in the last analysis all
> moments are key moments, and life itself is grace.
> (*Now and Then: A Memoir of Vocation*)

Some senses may not stay content with their job as information-conveyers, and attempt to become judges or even dictators; for example, we complain about socks that rub and labels that scratch. A highly-developed sense of hearing can be valuable in jobs that depend on the ability to hear tiny sounds or discriminate between tones; but it can also be a source of irritation and even pain. We have known a person with such an aural gift who was unable to stand the sound of rain on the roof. Likewise, an especially adept nose or tongue may lead to a career in wine-tasting or perfume-making, or it may simply turn someone into a picky eater.

Of course there are under-performing senses, sometimes for physical reasons. Charlotte was more concerned with those eyes, ears, and other senses that had nothing physically wrong with them, but that were still underdeveloped or underused. Many of her school subjects incorporated close observation or mental visualization. Children were taught to draw or sculpt the twigs or flowers in front of them, and to paint a scene from a story as they visualized it in their minds. They were encouraged to keep lists of birds they had seen, and to record the "firsts" of each season. They were taught to mentally store up their own views of the outdoor world, and to discover the ways that others had interpreted that world through visual art, music, poet, or even scientific discovery. Here we see the five senses at their finest, and used to their utmost—without any of them trying to be the boss.

> The world is a great treasure-house full of things to
> be seen, and each new thing one sees is a new
> delight. (p. 29)

> It must be a great disappointment / to God if we are
> not dazzled at least ten / times a day. (Mary Oliver,
> "Good Morning" in *Blue Horses*)

Scriptures to Ponder

> Consider the lilies how they grow: they toil not, they
> spin not; and yet I say unto you, that Solomon in all
> his glory was not arrayed like one of these. (Luke
> 12:27)

Along the Way

Make a list of ten ways that the world dazzles you today.

Day 10: From Body to Mind

> One thesis, which is, perhaps, new, that *Education
> is the Science of Relations*, appears to me to solve
> the question of a curriculum, as showing that the
> object of education is to put a child in living touch
> with as much as may be of the life of Nature and of
> thought. Add to this one or two keys to self-
> knowledge, and the educated youth goes forth with
> some idea of self-management, with some pursuits,
> and many vital interests. (Preface to *Ourselves*)

Did you notice what happened there? We have been talking about how
the Senses (in particular) put us "in living touch" with the world
around us, "the life of Nature," and to some extent "[the life] of
Thought" (through the art we see, the music we hear, and so on). Now
we begin to think of "education," "curriculum," "vital interests," and
"self-management." We seem to have trotted from the physical realm
into that which Charlotte calls the "Mind," or the "Inside Self":

> that still more wonderful Self which we cannot see
> and touch as we can our bodies, but which thinks
> and loves and prays to God; which is happy or sad,
> good or not good. (p. 33)

Each Desire of the Mind is discussed in its own chapter of *Ourselves*;
but, to begin with, we need to talk about the big leaders in the House,
Intellect and Imagination.

It is a good thing to discuss, as we have already, the workings of our
physical bodies, their appetites, their weaknesses. But those may seem
simple in comparison to the necessary, natural, but often conflicting
Desires that try to make themselves heard in the House of Mind.

Scriptures to Ponder

> Behold that which I have seen: it is good and
> comely for one to eat and to drink, and to enjoy the
> good of all his labour that he taketh under the sun
> all the days of his life, which God giveth him: for it
> is his portion... and yet the appetite is not filled. For

18

what hath the wise more than the fool? what hath
the poor, that knoweth to walk before the
living? Better is the sight of the eyes than the
wandering of the desire: this is also vanity and
vexation of spirit. (Ecclesiastes 5:18, 6:7-9)

Along the Way

Sunday Interlude #2

Professor Intellect is a busy man; his desk is covered with memos and
folders, all reminding him of the many things he should be doing in
the House of Mind. At the minute, however, he is feeling bored and
confined, "unwilling to begin to think of anything but the small
matters of everyday life." He's fed up to tears, bored to the teeth, and
can't even manage to keep his metaphors straight. Someone gives him
an equation to work on, and "Intellect bestirs himself, strong and eager
for his work…"; "yet the next time we come to the same fence,
Intellect jibs and we have to spur him to the leap; then all goes well"
(p. 45). And then again, and again.

Thinking that he might take on some extra research, he goes to see
the head of his department; but that office has been taken over by new
management from the Habit Corporation. Well, that explains that. We
have described Habit as a good servant, particularly in the House of
Body; but he can be more of a problem in the House of Mind.

> It is when he is allowed to play the bad master and
> override Intellect that he spoils and narrows life.
> Under Habit, Intellect cannot be said to be slothful;
> he goes briskly enough, but he goes over the same
> ground, day after day, year in, year out. The course
> may be a good one and it may be quite necessary to
> follow it. (pp. 45-46)

What is the remedy for Professor Intellect's autopilot status? He
doesn't like to be lazy, but it's as if one part of him says "Get to work,"
and the other says "Don't bother, what's the use?" His first thought is
that he needs to gain more Self-Control.

He calls up a colleague who, he has heard, went through much the same problem recently, and asks where or how Self-Control can be obtained. "It's not something that you can just order online," his friend says. "Before we can have Self-Control we must know a good deal about ourselves, that is, we must get Self-Knowledge." And where does one get that?

"You are in a rut, my friend. Habit's mistake is to keep you on the always on the same ground."

"But I do enjoy my work in physics," Intellect protests.

"It is possible for a person to go into any one of the great fields of thought, and to stay there with steady work and constant delight until he becomes incapable of finding his way into any other of these great fields. The happiness of the intellectual life comes of knowing and thinking, imagining and perceiving or rather, comes of the range of things which we know and think about, imagine and perceive.

"'To search, to endeavour, and to feel our way to a foothold from point to point is also exhilarating; and every step that is gained is a resting-place and a house of ease for Mansoul.' (p. 39) Therefore, the proper remedy for Intellect-on-autopilot is not so much a vacation as an adventure."

"An adventure? I don't know, this is a busy time. What did you have in mind, anyway?"

"Well, there was our friend Elwin Ransom's journey to Mars, although of course that was accidental. Any interest?"

Intellect shudders, but he tries to be polite. "That is perhaps a bit more than I had in mind; but some travels through the Self-Kingdom sound like just the right thing."

"Would you like some company?" his colleague says. "Perhaps I can take some time off to go with you. And I think Reason might be interested as well."

(The friend's name is Imagination. We'll hear more about him later on.)

But what does an office-bound Intellect need for a walking holiday? He phones down to the travel office, and the clerk there says she can easily supply him with a backpack of essentials, including a map. He asks if the contents can be customized, or if one can order a Deluxe pack instead of a Basic one, but she says no, they are all standard issue.

Professor Intellect is a little put out at that, as he likes to have choices, but the clerk explains:

> Many persons think themselves quite different from everybody else, which is a mistake. Self-knowledge teaches that what is true of everybody else is true of us also; and when we come to know how wonderful are the powers and how immense are the possibilities of Mansoul, we are filled, not with pride, but with Self-reverence, which includes reverence and pity for the meanest and most debased, because each of these is also a great Mansoul, though it may be a Mansoul neglected, ruined, or decayed. (p. 44)

Perhaps he's making a mistake with this venture? But when he remembers how dull life has been lately under Habit, he pulls his courage together and adds in an order, at least, for an extra-strong pair of boots. He also thinks about something else that Imagination said:

> It is our business to know all we can and to spend a part of our lives in increasing our knowledge of Nature and Art, of Literature and Man, of the Past and the Present. That is one way in which we become greater persons, and the more a person is, the better he will do whatever piece of special work falls to his share. Let us have... a spirit 'invariably royal and magnanimous.' (p. 47)

Scriptures to Ponder

> A wise man will hear, and will increase learning; and a man of understanding shall attain unto wise counsels... (Prov. 1:5)

Along the Way

Day 11: Intellect Goes Forth

We are now travelling through the Kingdom with Intellect,

21

Imagination, and a couple of other companions from the House of Mind. We've put on our hiking boots and gotten a good start on the road; but we must ask now, where are we headed? Intellect wants to begin with a place that is already familiar to him.

The Vast and Joyous Realm of Science

> Here, the stars are measured, the ocean sounded,
> and the wind made the servant of man; here, every
> flower that blooms reveals the secret of its growth,
> and every grain of sand recounts its history... the
> people who walk therein are always discovering new
> things, and each new thing is a delight, because the
> things are not a medley, but each is a part of the
> great whole. (p. 35)

Even though Intellect is a scientist, he complains that Science is such a big province that they can't possibly see everything. "That would take a lifetime, not a vacation. Maybe we should just stop for awhile and pick the pebbles out of our boots."

"Let's climb to the top of that hill," says Imagination. "Just past those trees. I can only imagine what we'll be able to see from there."

So they climb, and they are floored by the view of a huge canyon full of amazing rock layers and colours. Intellect has never seen anything like it, and he is grateful to Imagination for pushing them on. "You should be dubbed Lord Chief Explorer," he says to his colleague.

"Well," says Imagination, "Let it be said of us as it was of the Bishop of London, 'His was the rare gift of mastering knowledge as his splendid servant, not being himself mastered by it as its weary slave.'" (p. 44)

Climbing Higher in Mathematics

Mathematics is "a mountainous land, but the air is very fine and health-giving, though some people find it too rare for their breathing" (p. 38). Professor Intellect enjoys it; he says that "you cannot lose your way, and every step taken is on firm ground." Imagination enjoys the fresh air here too; but it is another companion, though, Reason, who comes into her own here as the guide of their explorations. (Her larger role in the kingdom will be discussed on **Day 15**).

Finding a Footing in Philosophy

> [The country of] Philosophy offers fascinating and
> delightful travelling, and the wayfarer here learns
> many lessons of life; but he does not find the same
> firm foothold as he whose way leads him through
> the Principality of Mathematics. Still, certainty is
> not the best thing in the world. To search, to
> endeavour, and to feel our way to a foothold from
> point to point is also exhilarating; and every step
> that is gained is a resting-place and a house of ease
> for Mansoul. (pp. 38-39)

Upwards and Outwards

Now we're getting into the deep woods, and there might be deer and
squirrels to spot. Or bears. There might be moss and trilliums to
examine. Or poison ivy. We take our chances.

Don't forget to look at the trees themselves: there are some
amazing birds up in those branches. Maybe even monkeys.

> ...if you realise at all what has been said, you will be
> surprised to know that many people live within
> narrow bounds, and rarely step into either of the
> great worlds we have been considering. The
> happiness of the intellectual life comes of knowing
> and thinking, imagining and perceiving or rather,
> comes of the range of things which we know and
> think about, imagine and perceive. (pp. 43-44)

Scriptures to Ponder

> I will fetch my knowledge from afar, and will
> ascribe righteousness to my Maker. For truly my
> words shall not be false: he that is perfect in
> knowledge is with thee. (Job 36:3-4)

Along the Way

Day 12: The Singing of Words (Imagination)

We have already heard how Imagination, now dubbed "Chief Explorer," encouraged Intellect to take this journey. But who is he?

Imagination is the videographer of Mansoul. His job is to "produce...a procession of living pictures in every region open to Intellect"; to make "pictures and poems...on the inner curtains of our minds"; and "collecting pictures of the great rich world."

> He is an amazing personage, with power to produce, as we have seen, a procession of living pictures in every region open to Intellect. Great artists, whether they be poets or painters, builders or musicians, have the power of expressing and showing to the rest of us some part, anyway, of the wonderful visions Imagination has revealed to them. But the reason why we enjoy their pictures, their poems, or their tales, is because Imagination does the same sort of thing for all of us, if in a less degree. (p. 48)

We tend to think of Intellect as a scholar hardly able to look up from his book or microscope; and Imagination also as an inward, introverted creature who wants to paint skies pink and trees purple; but it is when we look outward instead that both Intellect and Imagination flourish. Imagination gives us empathy for others, and even the ability to understand, though not to praise, the minds of those doing evil. He can show us ways we can serve others, or solve problems.

One way that Imagination gets off track is if he uses his talents to build "pleasure-houses for Self"; in current speech, turning the camera to Selfie mode. When we allow him merely to produce happy daydreams about ourselves and our own wonderfulness, we are not moving along the road at all, we are just "building pleasure-houses." Mentally picnicking, maybe, when there is work to be done. He may use his talents to produce horror movies or even pornography, and if these appear we need to quickly skip to the next video.

> If such terrors come at night, when you cannot do anything or read anything, you can always think of something else. The last story-book you have read,

24

for instance, —go over the tale in your thoughts. (p. 53)

The other danger of over-imagining our own importance (and beauty and goodness and cleverness) is that we must then (like Edmund in Narnia) under-imagine the value (and beauty and goodness and cleverness) of others, and in return they start to find us sulky and dull. Which is also "very provoking, because we know that all the time we have beautiful thoughts about what we shall do for every one of them, and the least they can do is to be kind meantime!"

What is a better response?

> A good plan is to take your Self by the shoulders, look him full in the face and laugh at him for a ridiculous fellow. This is what is called having 'the saving grace of humour,' and people who have it do not make themselves absurd by putting on airs and graces. (p. 51)

Imagination is one of the most deeply spiritual characters in the Kingdom, since our ability to *imagine* is one of the ways we are made in the *image* of God. If you "set this glorious servant to work in his rightful calling…you will be a delight to your friends, because you will have much to tell, and will be interested about many things." (p. 51)

Scriptures to Ponder

> Casting down imaginations, and every high thing that exalteth itself against the knowledge of God, and bringing into captivity every thought to the obedience of Christ (2 Corinthians 10:5)

Along the Way

Day 13: Where Imagination Takes Us

Imagination is most at home in the realms of History, Art, and Literature, and he is happy to guide his companions through these lands.

...when Intellect walks abroad in this fair kingdom,
he becomes intimate with the best of all ages and all
countries. Poets and novelists paint pictures for
him, while Imagination clears his eyes so that he is
able to see those pictures: they fill the world, too,
with deeply interesting and delightful people who
live out their lives before his eyes. (p. 39)

Lands of Literature

However, in a rather Bunyanesque image, Charlotte warns us of a
barren land on the borders of the kingdom of Literature. Like the field
of poppies just outside of Emerald City, we can be distracted or
seduced by its fragrance, never realizing that we are missing the real
thing. How can we tell the difference? Here is one way:

[It is a place] where pictures are painted for you and
where people are introduced; but you cannot see the
pictures with your eyes shut, and the people do not
live and act in your thoughts... (p. 40)

The second way is to listen to a passage, such as a poem, and ask if it
has "a certain charm in the wording which makes words go home to
our heart with living power." We notice this, for example, in translated
books, where one version may be technically correct, but seems to lack
a sense of rhythm or flow. This is why many English-speaking
Christians, no matter what their theological bent, find it easier to
memorize Scriptures from the King James Bible.

The thing is, to keep your eye upon words and wait
to feel their force and beauty; and, when words are
so fit that no other words can be put in their places,
so few that none can be left out without spoiling the
sense, and so fresh and musical that they delight
you, then you may be sure that you are reading
Literature, whether in prose or poetry. (p. 41)

(Much of the ability to appreciate that power depends not only on
Intellect and Imagination, but on another colleague travelling with
them. Charlotte calls him Beauty Sense; but I prefer to call him The
Connoisseur. He will be properly introduced tomorrow.)

Views of History

Have you ever seen an old movie where tourists on a beach are looking into a coin-operated viewer? Sometimes, long ago, those machines showed silent movies (they were called kinetoscopes). Other times, they were telescopes or spyglasses, so that people could look out at the water. The realm of History in Mansoul has some of each type, and our travellers pull out some coins and try them out.

Reason peers into a kinetoscope and complains that "many figures are there, living and moving, dancing, walking in procession, whatever they happened to be doing at the time the picture was taken, but very small and rather dim, and [the] most attentive gazing cannot make them clearer." (p. 36)

"Try just looking at one person," suggests Imagination; "the longer you look at him, the more clearly he will stand out." This, Reason finds, is true. They also come across a better viewing-glass, which shows "all the centuries and of every country full of a great procession of living, moving people…full of entertainment and sometimes of regret." The curious thing about this particular glass is that it can be taken off its stand and turned on those viewing it, so that they become part of the same moving picture.

"I understand!" says Reason. "We, too, are making History, and that we are all part of the whole; that the people who went before us were all very like ourselves, or else we should not be able to understand them. If some of them were worse than we, and in some things their times were worse than ours, yet we make acquaintance with many who were noble and great, and our hearts beat with a desire to be like them. That helps us to understand our own times."

Intellect responds, "We, too, live in a great age and a great country, in which there is plenty of room for heroes; and if these should be heroes in a quiet way, whom the world never hears of, that does not make much real difference. No one was ever the least heroic or good but an immense number of people were the better for it; indeed, it has been said that the whole world is the better for every dutiful life, and will be so until the end of time." (pp. 37-38)

Scriptures to Ponder

Finally, brethren, whatsoever things are true,

whatsoever things are honest, whatsoever things are
just, whatsoever things are pure, whatsoever things
are lovely, whatsoever things are of good report; if
there be any virtue, and if there be any praise, think
on these things. Those things, which ye have both
learned, and received, and heard, and seen in me,
do: and the God of peace shall be with you.
(Philippians 4:8-9)

Along the Way

Day 14: Paradise of Pleasure

Be Discerning

The chapter called "The Beauty Sense" describes the companion to
Intellect whom I have renamed The Connoisseur. He has a fine ear for
music and poetry, and an eye for art. On this journey, he is most
excited to visit the Palace of Art, where we meet others of his
acquaintance: Colour, Form, Proportion, and Harmony. Each room of
the house contains an example of beauty,

> ...[in] picture, statue, glorious cathedral, in delicate
> ornament, in fugue, sonata, simple melody. When
> we think for a moment, how we must admire the
> goodness of God in placing us in a world so
> exceedingly full of Beauty–whether it be of what we
> call Nature or of what we call Art–and in giving us
> that sense of Beauty which enables us to see and
> hear, and to be as it were suffused with pleasure at a
> single beautiful effect brought to our ear or our eye.
> (p. 42)

However, like the poor-copy poppy fields outside of the Kingdom of
the Literature, we can be fooled into knocking on the wrong door
when we go looking for Beauty.

> ...there [is] a dull and dreary Hall of Simulation

which we may enter and believe it to be the Palace of Art...the so-called artists labour away to get the colour and form of the things they see, and to paint these on canvas or shape them in marble or model them in wax (flowers), and all the time they miss, because they do not see, that subtle presence which we call Beauty in the objects they paint and mould. (p. 43)

But Don't Overdo It

The Connoisseur is a good companion for Intellect and Imagination, but he does not do well on his own. His charisma, and his refined tastes, can distract us from much that's interesting and worthwhile. Though so much else of this journey is about making choices, Charlotte says that, as in real life, there is much that we may *not* choose. We may not choose to exclude people because they are "unbeautiful"—or because their views don't please us. We may not choose to go only where we will not be bothered by ugliness and poverty. And we may not allow ourselves to be sidetracked off the main road by a never-ending search for an elusive Beauty.

In *Pilgrim's Inn*, a character named Nadine seems to exemplify this.

"Nadine—she can't help it, poor dear—was born a hungry, unsatisfied woman. Her perpetual search after perfection is a lovely thing in her; because of it her home and her person will never be less than exquisite, but it makes all the normal relationships disappoint her by their imperfection, so that she looks beyond them for happiness. At least she did until now. I think that perhaps, just lately, a glimmering of sense has been vouchsafed to her."

This is what was going on Nadine's own mind at that time:

Well, what next?...That hateful poem [by George Meredith] ...came to her mind. She had denied [her wrong desires]. Now she had to go out into that detestable wood and learn to laugh.

Charlotte's two suggestions for a healthy relationship with Beauty are not exactly the same, but they go in the same directions:

> In the first place, we must not let any better-than-
> my-neighbour notions get into our heads; and in the
> next, we must make it our business, as much as in
> us lies, to bring Beauty to places where it is not.

Not to take Beauty from others, but to offer it ourselves; and not in a condescending way, but simply, on an equal footing, and—when possible—with laughter.

Scriptures to Ponder

> To appoint unto them that mourn in Zion, to give
> unto them beauty for ashes, the oil of joy for
> mourning, the garment of praise for the spirit of
> heaviness; that they might be called trees of
> righteousness, the planting of the LORD, that he
> might be glorified. (Isaiah 61:3)

Along the Way

How important is Beauty to you? What are some ways we can find or create Beauty in the places around us, without allowing it to be an idol?

> She looked at the flowers with elation; their winter
> flowering, though it was so sparse and fragile, was
> so triumphant. To her left, a kingfisher flashed
> against the dazzle of the river, and she could have
> laughed aloud. She had shrunk from this wood, and
> now she found to her surprise that she was enjoying
> it. (*Pilgrim's Inn*)

Day 15: Let Us Reason

> ...the business of Reason is rather to prove for us
> that what we think is right, than to bring us to
> conclusions which are right in themselves... Your
> arrival at a right destination does not depend upon

> your choice of a good road, or upon your journeying
> at a good pace, but entirely upon your starting in
> the right direction. (p. 64)

Reason, the frequent companion of Intellect, is a lover of brain games. She is gifted with a microscope; can fit an impossible number of things into one suitcase; and can think quickly on her feet; she is someone we want to have on our side in a debate. Without Reason, a lot of things around us wouldn't make sense. She and Imagination together have invented many useful things. But she gets bored easily, and that's when she gets into trouble. Reason, striking out on her own or trying to act as a gatekeeper, has been responsible for a long list of human errors dating back to Genesis.

> Reason which is not worked grows sluggish; and
> there are persons who never wonder nor ask
> themselves questions about anything they see. (p.
> 65)

She sometimes likes to take the part of a Reformer, helping people "reason out the old things afresh" and bring them to a new understanding of how things work or how they could be run. Sometimes her conclusions are right, sometimes not; occasionally she has to be taken in hand by Common Sense, or by Love and Justice (governors of the House of Heart).

Reason also has a downside that, like a GPS in a car, she may be able to direct you from one point to another and tell you how long it will take and if you're going too fast, but she can't always tell you if you should be going there in the first place.

> All this time the Guard was looking at her, first
> through a telescope, then through a microscope,
> and then through an opera-glass. At last he said,
> "You're travelling the wrong way," and shut up the
> window and went away.
>
> "So young a child," said the gentleman sitting
> opposite to her (he was dressed in white paper),
> "ought to know which way she's going, even if she
> doesn't know her own name!"
>
> (Lewis Carroll, *Through the Looking Glass*)

Offering Ourselves

How can we make the best use of Reason in our Self-Kingdom? The first strategy is to give her plenty to do, of the sorts of things she is best at: for instance, "asking ourselves what is the cause of this and that; why do people and animals do certain things." Let her figure things out and put things together. The second is to understand that Reason has no right to speak the last word on most subjects, because (Lewis Carroll-like) the last word follows the lead of the first, and to speak the first word does not rest with her (p. 64). There are other governors in the Kingdom whose work is to examine ideas, to allow the proper ones across the borders, and to deport intruders if necessary.

And yet Reason can be an invaluable companion on the journey, if we keep her walking in the middle.

> The Queen propped her up against a tree, and said kindly, "You may rest a little now."
>
> Alice looked round her in great surprise. "Why, I do believe we've been under this tree the whole time! Everything's just as it was!"
>
> "Of course it is," said the Queen, "what would you have it?"
>
> "Well, in *our* country," said Alice, still panting a little, "you'd generally get to somewhere else—if you ran very fast for a long time, as we've been doing."
>
> "A slow sort of country!" said the Queen. (*Through the Looking Glass*)

Scriptures to Ponder

> To know wisdom and instruction; to perceive the words of understanding; To receive the instruction of wisdom, justice, and judgment, and equity; To give subtilty to the simple, to the young man knowledge and discretion. (Proverbs 1:2-4)

Along the Way

Day 16: Spotting the Great Speckled Desires

> ...one way or another, the Mind is sustained by the
> food it needs. (p. 68)

Charlotte names six Desires of the Mind, along with their associated "daemons," a.k.a. the potential dangers if they get out of hand or are used for wrong purposes. As we travel, we need to keep our binoculars handy to see them more clearly.

> It is as necessary that Mind should be fed, should
> grow and should produce, as that these things
> should happen to Body; and, just as Body would
> never take the trouble to feed itself if it never
> became hungry, so Mind would not take in what it
> needs, if it, also, had not certain Desires to satisfy.
> These gather the funds, as it were, for Mind, so we
> may amuse ourselves by calling them the Lords of
> the Exchequer. (p. 66)

What is the Exchequer? In British history, it was the government department responsible for collecting taxes or other funds, and deciding on public spending. The word "exchequer" comes from the Latin *scaccarium*, "chessboard," referring to the checkered cloth on which they counted up their money. Like the hypothetical piggybanks, the mind is always needing to be replenished!

Here's a cheat sheet of what to watch for:

Desire of Approbation (Praise, Approval of Others). Daemons: vanity; the desire of fame.

> ... all the time he is bringing grist to the mill,
> knowledge to the mind, because the people whose
> Approbation is worth having care that we should
> learn and know, conquer our idleness and get habits
> of steady work, so that our minds may be duly
> nourished every day as are our bodies. (p. 67)

Desire to Excel, or Emulation. Daemons: wanting things that are right and good in themselves, but letting Emulation get the upper hand; or wanting to be the best at something useless or harmful.

> Do you not know how another horse, in advance,
> puts yours on his mettle? It is as good as a prick of
> the spur to quicken his pace. And that is just what
> this Desire of Excelling does for us; it spurs us on to
> effort when we are lazy. (p. 68)

Desire of Wealth: Daemons: Selfishness and Avarice; Worthless Wealth, the desire to accumulate things of no real worth.

> [There is a] natural Desire of possessions
> implanted in Mansoul. But it rests with us that our
> possessions shall be worthy. (p. 71)

Desire for Power, a.k.a. Ambition. Daemons: wanting power for selfish reasons.

> Power is a good thing when it gives us many
> chances of serving; it is a bad thing when all we care
> about is to rule. (p. 71)

(There are two others yet to come.)

Scriptures to Ponder

> What profit hath he that worketh in that wherein he
> laboureth? I have seen the travail, which God hath
> given to the sons of men to be exercised in it. He
> hath made every thing beautiful in his time: also he
> hath set the world in their heart, so that no man can
> find out the work that God maketh from the
> beginning to the end. (Ecclesiastes 3:9-11)

Along the Way

Sunday Interlude #3

We will speak of another of the Mind's Desires:

The Desire for Society (The Company of Others)

> We want to see each other's faces, to hear each
> other's voices, to give pleasure to, and receive
> pleasure from, each other...then this natural Desire
> will do its [duty] in collecting sustenance for the
> mind.(pp. 73-75)

But as we journey, do we try to fall in step only with those who impress us, or who (we think) it would be a social boost to be seen chatting with (or to have following us on social media)?

> This is not only unmannerly and unkind, but is
> foolish, and a source of loss to themselves. Perhaps
> there is no one who has not some bit of knowledge
> or experience, or who has not had some thought, all
> his own.

Or do we try to do all the talking? Again, we miss out.

> ...intelligent listening is a very good viand for this
> table, and, what is more, a viand to everybody's
> taste. There are more people who can talk than who
> can listen. (p. 76)

What are the Daemons or risks here? One is letting Desire for Society take charge, which often squeezes out time better spent on other things ("all day chattering here and there, with nothing to show for it"). Another is wanting so much to be accepted that we listen to flatterers, to anyone who tells us we're wonderful. Or caring too much about getting "likes."

> He asked, moreover, if the Shepherds did not bid
> them beware of the Flatterer? They answered, Yes,
> but we did not imagine, said they, that this fine-
> spoken man had been he. (*The Pilgrim's Progress*)

Scriptures to Ponder

> And Ruth said, Intreat me not to leave thee, or to
> return from following after thee: for whither thou
> goest, I will go; and where thou lodgest, I will lodge:
> thy people shall be my people, and thy God my

God... (Ruth 1:16)

I am the vine, ye are the branches: He that abideth in me, and I in him, the same bringeth forth much fruit: for without me ye can do nothing. (John 15:5)

Along the Way

Day 17: The Best and Noblest (Desire for Knowledge)

Knowledge is what Charlotte calls the "noblest of our desires." It's been known to be one of the most dangerous desires out there (Genesis 2:17). But in the book of Proverbs, we're commanded to seek Wisdom. Proverbs 15:14 says that "the heart of him that hath understanding seeketh knowledge." We are made to want to know.

But what is Knowledge, and what is its purpose? To allow us to stuff our backpacks full of unconnected facts? No, as Charlotte's ninth principle states:

> We hold that the child's mind is no mere *sac* to hold ideas; but is rather, if the figure may be allowed, a spiritual organism, with an appetite for all knowledge. This is its proper diet, with which it is prepared to deal; and which it can digest and assimilate as the body does foodstuffs.

Let's stop walking there for a minute.

We've already discussed the importance of healthy and positive physical appetites, not spooked by daemons, but functioning in the way they were designed, as a proper diet for the body. Now we have "All Knowledge" as the proper diet of the mind. We have an appetite for it (which can be trained or restrained). We take it in at the proper time (we might say in a chaste way?), and we are thankful for all of it, whether it's plain bread and water or Easter ham and sweet potatoes.

And what happens when it becomes part of our "spiritual organism?"

> ...the person becomes what is called *magnanimous*,
> that is, a person of great mind, wide interests,
> incapable of occupying himself *much* about petty,
> personal matters...It is only in so far as Knowledge
> is dear to us and delights us for herself that she
> yields us lifelong joy and contentment. (p. 78, italics
> hers)

The love of Knowledge is, in itself, a good and natural thing. However, it can be displaced by "junk food": settling for mere curiosity and gossip; settling for knowledge as entertainment.

> It seems harmless enough to satisfy oneself with
> scraps of news about this notable person and the
> other, a murderer or a millionaire, a statesman or a
> soldier, a great lady or a dancing-girl—Curiosity is
> agape for news about any or all of them...Curiosity
> is satisfied to know something about a matter, and
> not really to know it. (p. 77)

Or by Emulation: we might say, envying the mind-meals that others share on their social media, or posting a great deal about our own breakfasts and dinners in the hopes of getting followers and "likes." The sunlight of Delight can get a bit clouded over and make it harder for us to pay attention to Knowledge walking along beside us. If we find ourselves reading even a good book just so we can cross it off our "challenge" list, maybe we need to reconsider our motives.

A Postscript on Knowledge

Having just written that bit about stuffing backpacks, I was amused to find that Charlotte had beaten me to it.

> **The Ordering of our Thoughts.**—We need not
> carry this little bit of knowledge about ourselves like
> a pack on our back. Once one knows a thing, it
> comes to mind when it is wanted, and is not a
> burden to think of all the time. (p. 80)

Scriptures to Ponder

The heart of him that hath understanding seeketh

37

knowledge: but the mouth of fools feedeth on
foolishness. (Prov. 15:14)

Along the Way

Day 18: A House Made of Love

Love and Justice are inseparable from Mansoul;
they are there, and we must take count of them. (p.
136)

As we moved almost imperceptibly from the House of Body into the
Realm of Mind, so we suddenly find we have arrived at the House of
Heart, or as we might also call it, the Moral Monastery. It is divided
into two houses, Love and Justice, each built about a day's journey
from the other.

We arrive first at the House of Love, and on knocking at the gate,
we are taken inside by a Porter. He tells us that we are welcome to stay
and enjoy the hospitality of the brothers, as the whole purpose of their
order is to bring happiness to Mansoul. Think about that.

All the great possibilities of Love are in every
human heart, and to touch the spring, one must
give Love. (p. 85)

He tells us the names of the ten hardworking brothers who have taken
their vows and earned the right to serve under Abbot Love: Pity,
Benevolence, Sympathy, Kindness, Generosity, Gratitude, Courage,
Loyalty, Humility, and Gladness. These may not be names that we
connect immediately with "happiness." But the Porter explains:

Have you ever thrown a stone into the water and
watched the circles about it spread?...It is as if, in
the first place, our home were the stone thrown in
to move our being; and from that central point the
circle of our love widens until it embraces all men.
No one, excepting our Lord Jesus Christ, ever knew
how much he could love, or how much he could do
for Love's sake... (pp. 81-82)

Once more, Love desires to give and serve; the gifts

38

and the service vary with the age and standing of
the friends; the child will bring the gift of
obedience, the parent may have to offer the service
of rebuke, but the thought of service is always
present to Love. (pp. 84-85)

Those Who Don't Quite Belong

There is a frequent visitor to the House of Love, called Self-Love. His
presence is often necessary, especially when it comes to the accounts
of the order and the maintenance of the building; but his interests are
not completely in tune with those of the ten brothers.

> His mind is so full of his own feelings and affairs
> that he has little time to think about those of other
> persons. He gives little love, and he deserves to get
> as little...(p. 82)

He often brings along his colleague Don't-You-Love-Me, who is even
less helpful because he is more demanding:

> [He] is irritable, offended, jealous, if he does not get
> the attention and affection he demands. He thinks it
> is because he loves this or that friend so dearly, but
> it is, in truth, because he loves himself that neither
> mother nor friend can give him all the love and
> consideration he seems to himself to deserve. (p.
> 83)

Another occasional visitor is The Trifler. He treats people as if he loves
them, especially in ways such as hugging and handing out Valentine's
Day cards, but he has no genuine loyalty or love. Occasionally he tries
to satisfy the requirements to join the order; but (like a camel stuck in
the eye of a needle) he decides that the rules are just too rigorous.

Scriptures to Ponder

We love him, because he first loved us. (1 John 4:19)

Along the Way

Day 19: Recognizing Love

Love is a pearl of price which every heart holds; but,
as many people pass counterfeits upon themselves
and upon their friends, it is well that we should
know how to recognise the jewel when we see it, and
above all when we feel, or think we feel it. (p. 83)

How do you recognize "the jewel" of genuine love? What are the giveaways that it is counterfeit?

Last Christmas, my husband and I went to a party where teams had to answer a trivia quiz. Our team correctly answered questions like "How many ghosts visited Ebenezer Scrooge" and "What is the word for the flappy skin on a turkey's neck," but, having barely if ever watched the 2003 film *Elf*, we were stumped by "What is the first rule in the Code of the Elves?" We suggested "Put sugar on everything," but that wasn't it. The correct rules are:

1. Treat every day like it's Christmas.
2. There's room for everyone on the nice list.
3. The best way to spread Christmas cheer is singing loud for all to hear.

These each hold some food for thought, and the fact that they are other-directed (if you read them that way) is commendable. The code set down by Abbot Love, by comparison, contains fewer candy canes, but no less sparkle:

Rule Number One: "Love delights in the goodness of another." Those who truly love influence others, by their words or their actions or just their manner, to be loving, to be unselfish, to serve others.

> To influence his friend towards unworthy ways
> would seem to Love like burning his own house
> about his head. (p. 84)

Rule Number Two: "Love seeks the happiness of his friend."

> ... and shrinks from causing uneasiness by fretful or
> sullen tempers, jealousy or mistrust. (p. 84)

Rule Number Three: "Love seeks to be worthy."

> ... he will himself grow in goodness for the pleasure

of his friend. (p. 84)

Rule Number Four: "Love desires to give and serve."

"Love not in word, neither in tongue," says the
Apostle, "but in deed and in truth..." (p. 85)

Note: there are a few characters who never make it past the door of
the House of Love, such as Coldness, Dislike, Aversion, and Hatred.
But they don't usually ask to come in anyway.

On **Day Two**, we mentioned Elizabeth Goudge's novel *The Dean's
Watch*, and the sense of God's love that sustained Miss Montague
through difficult times. By contrast, the watchmaker Isaac Peabody
and his sister Emma have been cut off from that knowledge, and are
little able to give love to others or to accept it for themselves. This
bitterness leads Emma, in particular, to commit acts of emotional and
even physical destruction. If you relate more to Isaac and Emma than
you do to cheerful elves or selfless monks, be assured that there's room
for everyone on the "love list." Here is one place to start:

It is only in the Love and the presence of God that
we can forgive injuries, and when we forgive, we
love. (p. 86)

And we will take the next few days to get to know each of the
brothers a little better.

Scriptures to Ponder

A new commandment I give unto you, That ye love
one another; as I have loved you, that ye also love
one another. (John 13:34)

Along the Way

Day 20: No Idle Tears (Pity and Benevolence)

Pity

Today we read about two of Abbot Love's ten brothers, Pity and

41

Benevolence. Pity is not a popular word these days, but it can be defined as Sympathetic Sorrow, an identification with the suffering or distress of others, and there is nothing patronizing or able-ist about that. As Charlotte says, though, we must allow Pity to stir us to action on behalf of those who suffer; otherwise all our tears

> ...are like the water of certain springs in the
> limestone which have the property of coating soft
> substances with stone...There are none so difficult
> to move to help as those who allow themselves the
> luxury of idle pity. (pp. 88-89)

And what is true of "idle pity" for others is equally true for ourselves. Charlotte says that "No tenant of the heart has alienated more friends or done more to banish the joys of life" than has Self-Pity. "A spot no bigger than a halfpenny may blot out the sun of our friends' love and kindness, of the whole happiness of life, and shut us up in a cold and gloomy cell of shivering discontent" (p. 90).

The antidote?

> The other and surer way of guarding ourselves from
> this evil possession is to think about others. Be
> quick to discern their pains and sufferings, and be
> ready to bring help. (p. 90)

Let us consider not only what our tears mean, but what God is telling us to do about them.

Benevolence

Charlotte here challenges us with a paradox: "It is usual to speak as if Benevolence meant nothing more than the giving of money or other help to persons in distress; but it is possible to give a great deal of such help without being benevolent, and to be benevolent without giving much material help." This seems to echo Jesus' comment in Luke 21 about the widow who gave her two small coins freely, vs. the richer people who gave more money "out of their wealth" but without the same love.

> There is no generosity in giving what we shall never
> miss and do not want; this is mere good-nature, and

is not even kindness, unless it springs out of a real
thought about another person's needs. (p. 104)

But now we must take it further. Benevolence, by definition, means
goodwill, sympathy, and a generosity of spirit (not just of the wallet).
We are to bear with the world as we *don't* like it, and we are to treat
those who irritate us, not with a superior or grudging attitude, but with
Benevolence. Brother Benevolence teaches us not just to put up with
the annoying ones, or to love them in some abstract and spiritual sense,
but to actually *like* them. And why must we do this?

> ...because all persons are born with the beautiful
> qualities of mind and heart we have spoken of, in a
> greater or less degree; and though the beauty of a
> person's nature may be like a gem buried under a
> dust-heap, it is always possible to remove the dust
> and recover the gem. (p. 91)

> ... all literature and all education are only useful so
> far as they tend to confirm this calm, beneficent,
> and therefore kingly, power—first, over ourselves,
> and, through ourselves, over all around us... (John
> Ruskin, "Lilies", in *Sesame and Lilies*)

And then Benevolence does one more paradoxical thing.

> He likes [people] too well to endure that they
> should spoil themselves by this or the other failing.
> He cannot endure either that people should grow up
> in ignorance, or that there should be sickness or
> suffering or friendlessness in the world; therefore
> his hands and heart are always busy with some
> labour of help. (pp. 92-93)

The Bad Boys

Brother Benevolence can't seem to turn around without being
obstructed by little daemons in monks' clothing. This week he kept a
list of them as they appeared, to help the other brothers tell the
difference and send them on their way.

Monday: Fastidiousness, a.k.a. Something Smells, who gets
offended at all ways which are not exactly his own. (The word

"fastidious" comes from the Latin word *fastidium*, meaning "aversion" or "disgust.")

Tuesday: Exigence, a.k.a. The Tinderbox: a touchy and prickly little person who watches for any slight or insult, however small or unintentional.

Wednesday: Censoriousness, a.k.a. The Critic: one who likes to blame but doesn't think of improving things.

Thursday: Selfishness, who tries to keep the whole House of Heart too busy to notice the needs of others.

Friday: Slothfulness, a.k.a. Good-Nature, takes matters pleasantly so long as he is not required to trouble himself about anything.

Saturday and Sunday: Tolerance and Indifference, who usually show up together. Tolerance resembles Good-Nature, but his specialty is never questioning people's *opinions* in the same way as Good-Nature does their *actions*. Good-Nature must not be mistaken for Goodwill.

How can we recognize genuine Benevolence? He doesn't just criticize; when he sees needs, he finds ways to fill them, without getting overly concerned about his own feelings. He often corresponds with Sister Candour from the House of Justice. Benevolence is gracious, but he wants to see people becoming their best selves, with health restored and relationships regained.

Scriptures to Ponder

> And though I bestow all my goods to feed the poor,
> and though I give my body to be burned, and have
> not charity, it profiteth me nothing. (1 Cor. 13:3)

Along the Way

Day 21: 100 Pounds of Thermal Concrete (Sympathy)

Compassion [or Sympathy] is the sometimes fatal
capacity for feeling what it's like to live inside

somebody else's skin. It is the knowledge that there can never really be any peace and joy for me until there is peace and joy finally for you too. (Frederick Buechner, *Wishful Thinking*)

Who is this Brother Sympathy? He is an empath, like Deanna Troi on *Star Trek: The Next Generation*, or Spock in the *Original Series* when he does a mind meld with some other creature.

[opening his mind-meld with the Horta]

Mr. Spock: [crying] AHH! PAIN! PAIN! PAIN! ("The Devil in the Dark")

And there, unfortunately, we do get an exaggerated impression of Brother Sympathy's sorrowful side. But he is also capable of great joy, and also of a sort of amazement that comes from being able to see into someone else's inner being. Charlotte says, perhaps anticipating Dr. Seuss, "It is as if the heart got room to expand" (p. 95).

Sympathy in Neutral

Just so does the would-be sympathiser reproach the cause of suffering and enfeeble the sufferer by weak pity, leading him to pity himself...[but] the hardness which attempts to brace him without sharing his suffering is hardly worse than this spurious sympathy; and it does less harm, because the false ring of it is more easily discerned. (p. 97)

Encouraging self-pity? Not so good. Equally unwelcome: a slap on a back that's already covered in poison ivy.

As he that taketh away a garment in cold weather, and as vinegar upon nitre, so is he that singeth songs to an heavy heart. (Prov. 25:20)

Sympathy in Reverse

If the purpose of Sympathy is to elevate and sustain, and if we participate in his work by believing in the best of people, then the reverse is also possible.

If we fail to give this Sympathy, if we regard the people about us as thinking small, unworthy thoughts, doing mean, unworthy actions, and incapable of better things, we reap our reward. We are really, though we are not aware of it, giving Sympathy to all that is base in others, and thus strengthening and increasing their baseness: at the same time we are shutting ourselves into habits of hard and narrow thinking and living. (pp. 96-97)

So no, we don't want to do that.

Just Listen

An attentive and deferential listener performs some of the highest offices of Sympathy; he raises and sustains the person to whom he listens, increases the self-respect of him who has done something, or seen something, or suffered something, which he wishes to tell. This is true service, because we all, 'even the youngest,' think too little of ourselves; and for that reason have not the courage of that which is possible to us. (p. 98)

And by doing that, we may just be able to pour 100 pounds of thermal concrete into someone's wound.

Mr. Spock: The Horta is badly wounded. It may die...

Captain James T. Kirk: Can you help it?

McCoy: Helped it? I cured it.

Kirk: How?

McCoy: Well, I had the ship beam down 100 pounds of that thermal concrete. You know, the kind we use to build emergency shelters out of 'em. It's mostly silicone. So I just troweled it into the wound, and it'll act like a bandage until it heals. Take a look. It's as good as new.

Scriptures to Ponder

[Charity] doth not behave itself unseemly, seeketh not her own, is not easily provoked, thinketh no evil; Rejoiceth not in iniquity, but rejoiceth in the truth... (1 Corinthians 13:5-6)

Along the Way

Day 22: Simple Kindnesses

We might think that Pity, Benevolence, and Sympathy would be enough to handle most of the work in the House of Love, and they do seem to take on the biggest jobs and get the most recognition. But Brother Kindness prefers to work behind the scenes, taking care of little every day needs that somehow escape the notice of the others. He mops the floor, feeds the cats, puts on more coffee, takes banana bread to the neighbours, waves out the window to children on their way to school. He notices that one of the older brothers could use a more comfortable chair, so he goes to a yard sale and scrounges not only a chair but a footstool. But the thing about Brother Kindness is that he has a very short memory, and there is no thought of keeping score. He does these small things for others without any "backward glance to see how the matter affects himself."

Think Kindly on Me

Brother Kindness has one other attribute: he likes to give people the benefit of the doubt. If we ask him why, he might simply quote the Golden Rule. When prodded for a better explanation, he thinks a minute and then says, "If I know I sometimes snap at someone not because I'm truly a mean person, but because three other impatient people before him finished off my own patience, then I need to allow that same possibility for others, for instance the unhelpful person behind the ticket counter. Maybe their feet hurt. Maybe they've missed their lunch. Maybe they had to work a longer shift than they expected to, and they're worried about someone at home. Or their boss has just spoken harshly to them, so they're taking it out on the customers." Kindness himself is a simple-hearted being who cannot imagine wanting to treat people with cruelty or maliciousness, so he attributes the same good motives to others.

And when he's wrong?

> [Then] our kind construction will have a double effect. It will, quicker than any reproof, convict our neighbour of his unkindness, and it will stir up in him the pleasant feelings for which we have already given him credit.

(Have you ever heard the story about the people who moved to a new town where they had heard everyone was friendly, and they found that to be true? And the other people who moved to a place where they were told that the inhabitants were mean and rude, and they found that to be true? And, of course, it was the same place?)

Scriptures to Ponder

> Charity suffereth long, and is kind; charity envieth not; charity vaunteth not itself, is not puffed up... (1 Corinthians 13:4)

Along the Way

Sunday Interlude #4

> Sympathy is an eye to discern, a lever to raise, an arm to sustain. The service to the world that has been done by the great thinkers—the poets and the artists—and by the great doers—the heroes—is, that they have put out feelers, as it were, for our Sympathy... (p. 96)

If a piece of art or music or poetry awakens our own Sympathy, then we should want to share that joy with others, believing that they will respond as we do, even if we don't know them personally. This, by the way, is one of the reassurances we have if we are called to teach a class or give a talk: that although we may not know everyone there or their experiences, we can believe in and draw on the human qualities that we all share. "If we have anything good to give, let us give it, knowing with certainty that they will respond." (p. 96)

> It becomes their lifetime quest to water new dreams. They become living examples of compassion, they become the answers to failure, they are the gifts of empathy... (Marva Collins, *Ordinary Children, Extraordinary Teachers*)

Scriptures to Ponder

> [Charity] beareth all things, believeth all things, hopeth all things, endureth all things. (1 Corinthians 13:7)

Along the Way

Sympathy is described as "an eye to discern, a lever to raise, an arm to sustain": all useful tools for a parent or teacher. So perhaps what we really need to practice "masterly inactivity" is—sympathy.

Day 23: Generosity, a Saving Grace

> We may understand the nature of this ruler of men better if we consider that what Magnanimity is to the things of the mind, Generosity is to the things of the heart. (p. 104)

To visualize Brother Generosity, think of Dickens' Ghost of Christmas Present.

> Its dark brown curls were long and free; free as its genial face, its sparkling eye, its open hand, its cheery voice, its unconstrained demeanour, and its joyful air... "You have never seen the like of me before!" exclaimed the Spirit. (Charles Dickens, *A Christmas Carol*)

How can we characterize him?

1. Brother Generosity is not a fawner, a flatterer, or boot-licker. He has enough self-respect not to worry about being popular with the "right" people.
2. He has friends of widely different types, because he is able to meet people where they are.
3. He is not on the lookout for others to give him what he thinks he is due. He deals fairly and generously himself, and trusts that people will treat him the same. Most often, they do.
4. He "walks serene in a large room" (p. 105). He is full of "large and warm thoughts of life and of our relations with one another" (p. 104).

George Bailey, in *It's a Wonderful Life*, is an example of a generous-spirited person. He spends much of his life struggling against his own nature, but it is that generosity of spirit which saves him in the end.

> It is a certain large trustfulness in his dealings,
> rather than the largeness of his gifts, or the freedom
> of his outlay, that marks the generous man. (p. 104)

Locking Up Generosity

The daemons have one particular tactic against Brother Generosity: they like to shut him in a small room where he cannot spread his crazy ideas about sharing from the heart and not asking much in return.

> [But every so often] some happy word or occasion
> lets him loose. When this happens to the whole
> community, we become alarmed and fear that we
> are all going mad; but really it is that we have
> suddenly burst into large living without the
> restraints proper to an accustomed way of life. (p.
> 106)

Generosity does care about people minding their own business and doing their share of the world's work. (See Nadine, below.) He just likes to see them reach out a little too.

> "[Mr. Fezziwig] has spent but a few pounds of your

mortal money: three or four, perhaps. Is that so much that he deserves this praise?"

"It isn't that," said Scrooge, heated by the remark... "Say that his power lies in words and looks; in things so slight and insignificant that it is impossible to add and count 'em up: what then? The happiness he gives is quite as great as if it cost a fortune." (*A Christmas Carol*)

What about the Herb of Grace?

In the season of Lent, it may seem odd to be using examples from Christmas stories, to discuss abundance and giving, when we began by recommending self-denial. Remember Elizabeth Goudge's character Nadine, who had to deny herself, and then go out to the woods (which she mistrusted and disliked), and learn to laugh? Nadine struggled to love her husband (he was a good man, but a little dull), and even her children. She needed to experience self-denial to say no to the daemons who teased her with the idea that there was something better out there. But she also needed to feel what Charlotte calls "a generous impulse...which causes [someone], if only for a moment, to live outside of their own lives" (p. 103).

> That which seems to us our business in life, even that incessant business of being the mother of a family, will be far better done if we rule ourselves in this matter, because we shall be better, broader persons; and the more there is of a person, the more work will be done. (p. 106)

Scriptures to Ponder

> Who, being in the form of God, thought it not robbery to be equal with God: But made himself of no reputation, and took upon him the form of a servant, and was made in the likeness of men: And being found in fashion as a man, he humbled himself, and became obedient unto death, even the death of the cross. (Philippians 2:6-8)

51

Along the Way

Day 24: Let Heaven and Nature Sing (Gratitude)

> Life would be dull and bare of flowers if we were not
> continually getting more than we can pay for either
> by money or our own good offices; but a grateful
> heart makes a full return, because it rejoices not
> only in the gift but in the giver. (p. 109)

> To make use of other people, to serve ourselves of
> them, is the sin of ingratitude. (p. 110)

Meet Brother Gratitude. He's a happy servant in the House of Love, but he's more complicated than he first appears. Charlotte sets up a little scenario as an example:

> You go into a shop, and the shopkeeper who knows
> you...adds a pleasant something to your purchase
> which sends you cheerily on your way—some little
> kindness of look or word, some inquiry that shows
> his interest in you and yours, perhaps no more than
> a genial smile, but you have got into pleasant
> human relations with him because he has given you
> a kindness. (p. 109)

Let's update the shopkeeper to a coffee shop barista. So you drive through or you come out the door with your large coffee with your name written on the cup and extra cinnamon or whatever sprinkled on top, and there's maybe even a little paper cup of whipped cream for your dog (it's a thing). Brother Gratitude, riding shotgun or walking beside you, asks a question: "Do you feel as if you deserved that extra attention because you are such an important person, or because you were wearing a cool outfit today, or because your kids are so cute?"

> The joy [should be] not merely that we have
> received a favour or a little kindness which speaks

52

of goodwill and love, but that a beautiful thing has
come out of some other person's beautiful heart for
us; and joy in that other's beauty of character gives
more delight than any gain or pleasure which can
come to us from favours. (p. 108)

[The recipient should] go away with the springing
gladness of a grateful heart, knowing that he takes
with him more than he has bought. (p. 109)

Did you notice the quote at the beginning of this reading? We are
thankful for the gift; but we rejoice just as much or more in the giver.
We are thankful for them, "that a beautiful thing has come out of some
other person's beautiful heart for us."

Brother Gratitude likes to mark these small events in his own way.
He keeps a garden at the House of Love, full of flowers, but not all in
organized rows and proper beds. Brother Gratitude's flowers "bloom
unawares," any time a kindness has been shown. And these are no
ordinary flowers: they are not just beautiful to look at, and with a
beautiful scent, but if you put your ear close to them, you can hear
them singing.

Brother Gratitude has permission to leave the House as needed,
and he often walks along the roadways and the streets of the nearby
village, scattering seeds as he goes, so that the flowers can come up at
any time. As visitors to the monastery garden delight in the always-
changing blooms there, so the people of the village have learned to
watch for them springing up (and sometimes surreptitiously try to
make a few extras bloom by treating each other with extra kindness).

...to be on the watch for such flowers adds very
much to our joy in other people, as well as to the
happy sense of being loved and cared for. (pp. 108-
109)

And Don't Forget the True Giver

Every good gift and every perfect gift is from above,
and cometh down from the Father of lights, with
whom is no variableness, neither shadow of turning.
(James 1:17)

Scriptures to Ponder

> ...giving thanks always for all things unto God and the Father in the name of our Lord Jesus Christ... (Ephesians 5:20)

> Rooted and built up in him, and stablished in the faith, as ye have been taught, abounding therein with thanksgiving. (Colossians 2:7)

Along the Way

Day 25: Life is Like a Tin of Courage

> ...the form of Courage which meets pain and misfortune with calm endurance is needed by us all. No one escapes the call for Fortitude, if it be only in the dentist's chair. It is well to be sure of ourselves, to know for certain that we have Courage for everything that may come, not because we are more plucky than others, but because all persons are born with this Lord and Captain of the Heart. Assured of our Courage, we must not let this courage sleep and allow ourselves to be betrayed into panic by a carriage accident or a wasp or a rat. (p. 113)

We know what Courage is, especially in its common forms of Endurance and Serenity. We may know that it comes from the Latin *cor*, heart. To be dis-couraged is to be dis-heartened. We probably even have our favourite examples of great courage, or Scriptures or poetry about it.

> Fear thou not; for I am with thee: be not dismayed; for I am thy God: I will strengthen thee; yea, I will help thee; yea, I will uphold thee with the right hand of my righteousness. (Isaiah 41:10)

The Daemons of Courage are also obvious: Fear (accompanied by Panic and Anxiety), Timidity, and Cowardice. But how do we keep them under control? As we rummage in our backpack, we pull out something that looks like a tin of biscuits, labelled "Courage. One serving is enough for the present without any fearful looking forward." That is, we need to look only at the next step, the next thing, the next hour, whether we are facing something deeply grievous or just something that may or may not turn out well. The one who gave us trust and courage has commanded us to use it, and we must obey.

> Pardon for sin and a peace that endureth
> Thine own dear presence to cheer and to guide;
> Strength for today and bright hope for tomorrow,
> Blessings all mine, with ten thousand beside!
>
> (Thomas O. Chisholm, "Great is Thy Faithfulness")

Special Kinds of Courage

We open our box of Courage and realize that these are, indeed, mixed biscuits. Charlotte names several varieties besides those already named:

The courage of our opinions

To be shared with calmness and conviction. (More on this on **Day 35.**)

The courage of frankness

To be shared with trust.

The courage of reproof

To be shared with delicacy and gentleness (these biscuits crumble easily).

The courage of confession

To be shared sparingly, as confession is not always helpful to the person receiving it, especially regarding thoughts and feelings.

The courage of our capacity and the courage of opportunity

To be eaten of freely, with the words "I am, I can, I ought, I will."

55

Scriptures to Ponder

> Have not I commanded thee? Be strong and of a
> good courage; be not afraid, neither be thou
> dismayed: for the Lord thy God is with thee
> whithersoever thou goest. (Joshua 1:9)

Along the Way

The problem with fear, in many situations, is not only that being the stressed, anxious one makes us feel embarrassed, but that it keeps us from being of use to others, and we may pass our stress on to them as well. Charlotte has a rather blunt, Cousin-Ann-like response. (If you don't know Cousin Ann yet, please read *Understood Betsy*.)

> Let us possess ourselves and say: 'What does it
> matter? All *undue* concern about things and
> arrangements is unworthy of us.' It is only persons
> that matter; and the best thing we can do is to see
> that one person keeps a serene mind in unusual or
> fretting circumstances; then we shall be sure that
> one person is ready to be of use.

Can you be that one person who passes out the courage biscuits (instead of passing out)?

Day 26: Loyalty is a Sticky Thing

When our children were small, we used to sing a song that went "Sticky bubble gum, sticking your hands on your knees" or "your feet to the floor." Loyalty, like bubble gum or a roll of duct tape, is what sticks us to a place, to a leader, to our friends and relatives, even to tradition, beliefs, ways of doing things. We may love and approve of the ones we're loyal to; or we may barely tolerate them, not like their decisions much at all.

> The strength, grace, and dignity of a constant mind
> is the ingathering of Loyalty. (p. 123)

The thing about loyalty, though, is that it's not whatever we come up with at the time. We may have our loyalties stuck on us without our asking for them, and, as Charlotte says, we don't often get to ask for some other colour or flavour; the question is simply how well we will serve them. She points out that, even in the case of an undeserving monarch, the knight may gain more by his loyalty than the king does.

> "Thimbles and thunderstorms!" cried Trumpkin in a rage. "Is that how you speak to the King? Send me, Sire, I'll go."

> "But I thought you didn't believe in the Horn, Trumpkin," said Caspian.

> "No more I do, your Majesty. But what's that got to do with it?...You are my King. I know the difference between giving advice and taking orders. You've had my advice, and now it's the time for orders."

> (C.S. Lewis, *Prince Caspian*)

Every Yes Means Another No

> The same principles of Loyalty apply to Loyalty to our work and to any cause we have taken up. Thoroughness and unstinted effort belong to this manner of Loyalty; and, therefore, we have at times to figure as unamiable persons because we are unable to throw ourselves into every new cause that is brought before us. We can but do what we are able for; and Loyalty to that which we are doing will often forbid efforts in new directions. (p. 124)

In other words, that bubble gum will stretch only so far. Sometimes loyalty means under- rather than over-commitment. We can only do a certain amount well, and sometimes we have to be "unamiable" and say no to the rest. Certain wise preachers have said that even Christ-honouring tasks must be done by those who are called to do them.

It does happen that sometimes we have to leave a group, end a relationship, or change plumbers. And, occasionally, it comes about that "right-thinking people can no longer be loyal to king *and* country; when unjust laws, undue taxes, the oppression of the poor, make men's hearts sore for their fatherland." We may have to fight for justice in our own country, or even begin again in a new place. We can only pray for guidance to know when such a breaking off is right, and for the compassion and wisdom to do so without adding more harm to what has already been done.

Stirring up the Selfs

The daemons which most often trail after Brother Loyalty are those of Self: Self-Interest, Self-Conceit, and Self-Importance. Their biggest trick is "spoofing" his cell phone number. We may get texts pretending to be from Loyalty, but they're really from one of the Selfs. Self-Interest: "I know she's your friend, but there is only one spot open, and even though she said she was interested it's more important that you shouldn't miss out." Self-Conceit: "She insulted you in front of the boss, even if she said she didn't mean to, and she doesn't deserve to be your friend." Self-Importance: "I know she had the idea first, but you did a lot of the work. Well, she did most of the computer part, but that's because she's good at it. And anyway you are a senior member of the Punkadunk Women's Club, so she should have let you take the credit for the slideshow." You know what to do: delete, delete.

But you still wish for something better, something real. Take courage, Charlotte says:

> These enemies be about us, but Loyalty *is* within us,
> strong and steadfast, and asking only to be
> recognised [so] that he may put the [enemies] to
> flight. (p. 125)

Scriptures to Ponder

> The first of all the commandments is, Hear, O
> Israel; The Lord our God is one Lord: And thou
> shalt love the Lord thy God with all thy heart, and
> with all thy soul, and with all thy mind, and with all
> thy strength: this is the first commandment. And
> the second is like, namely this, Thou shalt love thy
> neighbour as thyself. There is none other
> commandment greater than these. (Mark 12:29-31)

Along the Way

Day 27: Getting Over Ourselves (Humility)

> [1 John 2:16] points out three causes of offence in men—the lust of the flesh, that is, the desire to satisfy the cravings of what we call 'human nature'; the lust of the eye, which makes the pursuit of the delight of beauty, not a part, but the whole of life [**Day 14**]; and, the pride of life. Of the three, perhaps, the last is the most deadly, because it is the most deceitful.

Most of us are taught from a young age that greed is not only displeasing to God but somewhat anti-social: we've all watched or read some version of *A Christmas Carol.*And not many of us, Charlotte suggests, are prone to lose our spiritual cool over "the delight of beauty." But Pride: that's the one that sneaks up on us, and it sometimes deceives us through Brother Humility—or a warped, travestied version of him True Humility, Charlotte says, is "gracious and beautiful, strong to subdue." He is never about saying "I can't." Humility does not allow us to refuse to risk failure or look foolish. He does not exempt us from the call to do hard things bravely. Think of Moses facing Pharaoh. Think of Christian on his journey. Think of small hobbits.

But because Humility can be thought to be so Uriah-Heepish, we may turn the other way, and become proud of whatever doesn't lump us with all the humble hypocrites.

> I guess you could say I'm a loner
> A cowboy outlaw, tough and proud
> Well, I could have lotsa friends if I wanted
> But then I wouldn't stand out from the crowd
>
> (Mac Davis, "Hard to be Humble")

We can find ourselves secretly hanging onto a hot temper, for example, because it keeps us "real." Or we nurture some ugly thing on our shoulder like "a little red lizard…whispering things in [our] ear" (C.S. Lewis, *The Great Divorce*).

"Be careful," it said. "He can do what he says. He
can kill me. One fatal word from you and he *will*!
Then you'll be without me for ever and ever. It's not
natural. How could you live?"

Not natural? That's hitting below the belt. Thankfully, Scripture has a
response:

...the natural man receiveth not the things of the
Spirit of God: for they are foolishness unto him:
neither can he know them, because they are. (2 Cor.
2:14)

But the biggest reason for holding pridefully onto anything—
physical possession, intellect, opinion, good work, even sin—is
because it's *ours*. The only way to let Humility work is to take the focus
off *me, mine, ours, us, we*. Even *trying* to be humble is a mistake.

How do we avoid both false humility and pride? First of all,
Charlotte says, we need to watch how often we use words like "I" in
conversation and writing, even if we include a "Thou," as in, "My best
friend." But what should we think or talk about instead? It seems that
almost any subject will do, but Charlotte names some of Brother
Humility's favourites:

... the love and knowledge of birds and flowers, of
clouds and stones, of all that nature has to show us;
pictures, books, people, anything outside of us... (p.
129)

Any of those should keep our brains busy enough to quell the little red
ego monster. (And fun for kids too.)

Scriptures to Ponder

But the wisdom that is from above is first pure, then
peaceable, gentle, and easy to be intreated, full of
mercy and good fruits, without partiality, and
without hypocrisy. (James 3:17)

Take my yoke upon you, and learn of me; for I am
meek and lowly in heart: and ye shall find rest unto
your souls. (Matthew 11:29)

Along the Way

Try writing a letter to someone that includes as many interesting objective details as possible, for instance about the things you saw on a walk. In other words, not too much "I."

Day 28: Serving with Gladness

Charlotte uses at least two separate metaphors to describe the work of Brother Gladness. One is that when he's around, things go better; without gladness, we are like "sad" bread that doesn't rise well. Which is something that can happen to anyone's baking, on a damp day or when the gremlins are out; but bread dough doing its proper thing should be the norm. If it often bakes heavy and flat, we need to look at what's in it, if our flour's good and our yeast is fresh, if we put in the salt and the right amount of liquid, if it's rising in a spot that's just warm enough, and or if someone's coming along and punching it down when they shouldn't. And to update the reference, maybe the bread machine is broken. In any case, that's not okay. If we mix flour and liquid and yeast or starter, we should expect to see dough that rises up.

> Another parable spake he unto them; The kingdom
> of heaven is like unto leaven, which a woman took,
> and hid in three measures of meal, till the whole
> was leavened. (Matthew 13:33).

> We laugh now and then, we smile now and then, but
> the fountain of Gladness within us should rise
> always; and so it will if it be not hindered. (p.132)

The second thing Brother Gladness is good at—or that is sometimes needed for him to work freely—is unplugging, cleaning out waste and junk. (It may go either way.) Have you ever read Eleanor Farjeon's story "San Fairy Ann?" While it's not meant as an allegory, there are a number of parallels. During World War II, Cathy Goodman is evacuated from London to a small village called Little Eggham. As the story begins, she has been there for some time, and she is a problem.

> She didn't fit in. She didn't try to. She had no

> parents and seemed to belong to nobody; ever since
> she had come to Little Eggham she had got the
> habit of being unhappy, and resisted all attempts at
> friendliness... ("San Fairy Ann," in *The Little
> Bookroom*)

In addition to all the trauma that might be expected of an orphaned, uprooted little girl, Cathy's precious doll, San Fairy Ann, had been thrown to the bottom of the village pond during a fight with another child. Nobody else knew about this particular grief, and Cathy had never told what happened; everyone just thought she was an exceptionally bad-tempered child.

> Somebody has trodden on our toe, somebody has
> said the wrong word, has somehow offended our
> sense of self-importance, and behold! the Daemon
> of self-pity digs diligently at his rubbish-heap, and
> casts in all manner of poor and paltry things to
> check the flow of our spring of Gladness. (p. 134)

But, finally, two women decide to clean out the drought-ridden, smelly pond full of soup tins, old boots, and chair legs. And then good things start to happen for everyone.

> ... remove the rubbish, and Gladness will flow out of
> the weary heart as freely as out of the child's. (pp.
> 131-132)

Rules of Gladness

While we have sympathy for Cathy and all she went through, we must also look beyond circumstances, good or bad as they may be, for a glimpse of Brother Gladness; especially if we want him to be more than an occasional visitor.

> Let us get the good out of our circumstances by all
> means, but as a matter of fact it is not our
> circumstances but ourselves that choke the spring.
> (p. 134)

Someday our own sunken treasures may be unearthed. But until then, we need to allow Gladness to flow out to others, in spite of all the table legs and sardine cans that may have been thrown into the pond.

> ...there is in each of us a fountain of Gladness, not
> an intermittent but a perennial spring, enough and
> to spare for every moment of every year of the
> longest life, not to be checked by sorrow, pain, or
> poverty, but often flowing with the greater force and
> brightness because of these obstructions ... (p. 133)

Scriptures to Ponder

> Rejoice in the Lord always: and again I say, Rejoice.
> (Philippians 4:4)

> Serve the Lord with gladness: come before his
> presence with singing. (Psalm 100:2)

Along the Way

Maybe bake something with yeast, or at least with baking powder? And think about rising.

Sunday Interlude #5

We have spent a long time visiting in the House of Love, and it is now time for us to travel to its sister abbey, the House of Justice. We should arrive there on Monday; but we will spend our Sunday "Little Easter" in a place of refreshment, sitting by the Stream of Consciousness.

Charlotte Mason wrote about the importance of the affinities we form in childhood: the connections and relationships, long-running threads, and, yes, loyalties. When I was reading about the Victorian designer/poet/reformer William Morris, a number of those affinities became apparent. We know that Morris developed an early love of nature, for example the Thames river and the willows that grew along its banks, and later the garden flowers that inspired so many of his designs. There was also his affinity for Scott's *Waverley* novels: he claimed to have read them all before he was nine years old. And there was art: when he was eight, his father took him to Canterbury Cathedral to see the stained-glass windows, and he said he felt the gates of Heaven had been opened to him.

Some of you may know Robert Macfarlane's children's book *The Lost Words*, which he wrote as a lament for our increasing inability not just to interact with the natural world, but to speak about it as well. In one of his adult books, *Landmarks*, he says almost the same thing:

> "Our language for nature is now such that the things
> around us do not talk back to us in ways that they
> might. As we have enhanced our power to
> *determine* nature, so we have rendered it less able
> to *converse* with us."

One of William Morris's goals was to find out how not only the natural but the human-made things might "converse with us." He wondered, for instance, could an everyday object like a chair be a piece of art? Should it be? Did it matter what it was made of, or where those materials came from, or who put it together, under what sort of working conditions? How did the chair fit into the rest of the room? And how did he reconcile the fact that many of his firm's workers couldn't afford the chairs or other products they sold? The answer to that last question is, he hated it, but he also didn't want to cut corners and reduce the quality of his products.

> Indeed, this sort of care not to do bodily hurt to
> other people should guide us in many of the affairs
> of life—should, for example, forbid us to buy at the
> cheapest shops; for most likely some class of work-
> people have been 'sweated' to produce the cheap
> article. A fair sense of the value of things helps us
> much in leading the just life. (pp. 141-142)

> What we want is—not the best thing that can be had
> at the lowest possible price—but a thing suitable for
> our purpose, at a price which we can afford to pay
> and know to be just. (p. 176)

Morris himself would certainly have pointed to the way he was influenced in his university years by the writer and artist John Ruskin, whose book *The Stones of Venice* was extremely popular right then. Ruskin was a reviver of Gothic architecture. He promoted a return to craftsmanship, the kind that was carried out in the medieval guilds; finding joy in one's work; and creating usefulness without selling out to utilitarianism. Morris and his cohort tried to look at art in a holistic way, asking not whether something that was created was meant to live in a frame on the wall, or if it had a practical purpose such as a floor covering, but rather if it showed true beauty, and if it related to human life—if it conversed with us.

> "I am not saying these things in blame of you, dear Prince," answered the Doctor. "You may well ask why I say them at all. But I have two reasons. Firstly, because my old heart has carried these secret memories so long that it aches with them and would burst if I did not whisper them to you. But secondly, for this: that when you become King you may help us, for I know that you also, Telmarine though you are, love the Old Things."
>
> "I do, I do," said Caspian. "But how can I help?"
>
> "You can be kind to the poor remnants of the Dwarf people, like myself. You can gather learned magicians and try to find a way of awaking the trees once more. You can search through all the nooks and wild places of the land to see if any Fauns or Talking Beasts or Dwarfs are perhaps still alive in hiding." (*Prince Caspian*)

As I have said, Morris was often frustrated by how contradictory his business life seemed to be. But his gift was to create beautiful things; he couldn't keep away from that. In the early 1880's, he created new textile designs based on tributaries of the Thames, the river that he had loved all his life. Perhaps that was his own way of "awaking the trees."

So find something…a natural thing, an Old Thing, a forgotten thing… to attach yourself to. Incorporate it into the design of your life, let it converse with you, and stand up for it as needed. Stay in tune with your own river. Because those things are also "loyalty."

Scriptures to Ponder

> The heavens declare the glory of God; and the firmament sheweth his handywork. Day unto day uttereth speech, and night unto night sheweth knowledge. There is no speech nor language, where

their voice is not heard. (Psalm 19:1-3)

Along the Way

Day 29: The House of Justice

After a long walk along the road to the House of Justice, we arrive at its gate, set in a high stone wall. A Porter answers our knock with a not-very-welcoming message: "There is no need for you to come in; and we require a toll from those who do." We respond, "But we've travelled a long way to find Justice!" The Porter replies,

> ... there is not a Mansoul in the world, however
> mean or unconsidered, neglected or savage, who
> has not justice in his heart. A cry for fair-play will
> reach the most lawless mob. 'It's not fair,' goes
> home to everybody. (p. 137)

However, we have learned much from Brother Humility, and we respond, "It is quite plain that to think fairly, speak truly, and act justly towards all persons at all times and on all occasions, which is our duty, is a matter requiring earnest thought and consideration—is, in fact, the study of a lifetime." (p. 138)

"Then you are welcome," the Porter says, "provided you are also willing to pay the toll for those that came here just ahead of you." We now see that there is a whole family standing off to one side, but looking anxious, as if they are waiting to get in but cannot afford it. We are not sure that we have enough money for ourselves and them as well, but we reach into our pockets...

> and behold! we have in hand always that coin of the
> realm of justice wherewith to pay the dues of all our
> neighbours. (p. 138)

So we all go in together.

What is Justice?

> [Mrs. Bedonebyasyoudid] had on a black bonnet,
> and a black shawl, and no crinoline at all; and a pair
> of large green spectacles, and a great hooked nose,
> hooked so much that the bridge of it stood quite up
> above her eyebrows; and under her arm she carried
> a great birch-rod. Indeed, she was so ugly that Tom
> was tempted to make faces at her: but did not; for
> he did not admire the look of the birch-rod under
> her arm.

(Mrs. Bedonebyasyoudid then talks to Tom)

> "I am very ugly. I am the ugliest fairy in the world;
> and I shall be, till people behave themselves as they
> ought to do. And then I shall grow as handsome as
> my sister, who is the loveliest fairy in the world; and
> her name is Mrs. Doasyouwouldbedoneby. So she
> begins where I end, and I begin where she ends; and
> those who will not listen to her must listen to me, as
> you will see."

(Charles Kingsley, *The Water-Babies*)

When we meet Mother Justice, the head of this House, she is carrying, not a birch rod, but four large books. The first is titled *Distributive Justice* (who gets what). The second book is titled *Procedural Justice* (how to treat people fairly). The third is a large black volume titled *Retributive Justice* (punishment for wrongdoing). The fourth is titled *Restorative Justice* (restored relationships). Some people think Justice is concerned only with punishing misbehaviour, like Mrs. Bedonebyasyoudid; but she is a person of wide interests, and once you get to know her, she is as beautiful as Mrs. Doasyouwouldbedoneby.

Who needs Justice?

Every person we come in contact with has the right to expect justice from us. Those in authority over us. Those serving us. Those who are our equals. Those we like, and those we don't.

I must be fair, that is, just, to all persons whose
opinions and ways of life differ from my own, even
to all who offend against the laws of God and man.
It is my duty to be just in this way to the persons,
the reputation, and the property of all other
persons, so far as I have anything to do with them.
(p. 138)

Tomorrow's reading will discuss some ways of carrying out that desire
for Justice.

Scriptures to Ponder

He hath shewed thee, O man, what is good; and
what doth the LORD require of thee, but to do
justly, and to love mercy, and to walk humbly with
thy God? (Micah 6:8)

Along the Way

Day 30: "To All Persons"

What does Charlotte mean by "justice to persons?" Later readings will
deal with being just in our speech, in our thoughts, and so on; but this
first challenge, she says, is to treat others according to their personal
rights, to what is "due" them. It is the Golden Rule, the Common Law,
nothing new, in fact very old.

But this often requires slowing down, looking at what's going on
around us, and using our imaginations to think about how our actions
might help or hurt others. Are we, in some way, making extra work for
others? Is our expectation of quick service or extra space
inconveniencing someone else? Do we, so to speak, leave a mess
behind us for someone else to clean up? Are we allowing the
"Daemons" of Thoughtlessness, Selfishness, or even Cruelty to creep
in? If so, we need to stop that. As Robert Fulghum once wrote, "Put
things back where you found them," "Don't take things that aren't
yours," and "Flush." 'Nough said.

[Mother] Justice, holding court within, ordains that

we shall think fair thoughts of everybody, near or
far, above or below us. When we are minded to
think fairly, [s]he has [her] group of servitors at our
command, whose business it is to attend to this very
matter and to come at call when they are wanted.
(pp. 143-144)

The Sisters of Justice

See, now, how the servitors of Justice stand by one
another! Candour, we have seen, is accompanied by
Respect, and Respect is supported by Discernment.
(p. 147)

Sister **Candour** has a gift for us: "glasses of unusual power, to bring
far things near and make dim things clear. Wearing these, we can see
round the corner, to the other side of the question." These glasses offer
us insight and compassion; they give others the same benefit of the
doubt as we would like to have it offered to ourselves. Now, a tricky
person named Prejudice sometimes sneaks into the House wearing a
nun's habit, and mixes her own glasses in with those of Candour; so
we have to be on the watch for that. One way to recognize true
Candour is that she is usually accompanied by Sister Respect.

...every [adult] and every child calls for our
honour... because Love and Justice, Intellect,
Reason, Imagination, all the lofty rulers of Mansoul,
are present, however dormant, in every [person] we
meet. (p. 146)

Does that mean that every person should be our close friend? No,
because behind those others we see a quiet but sharp-eyed sister named
Discernment.

We owe honour to all men; but Discernment steps
in to help us to do justice to ourselves, and choose
for our intimacy, or service, those whose characters
should be a strength to our own. (p. 147)

Consider what Charlotte is saying there. An exuberant spendthrift
might be the perfect best friend (or life partner) for a shy person who
can afford to have a little more fun, but he could be disastrous for

someone with an empty credit card and no self-control. The point is usually not that someone is worthy of *nobody's* close friendship—it just might not be yours. Dana K. White says that we need to determine our personal "clutter threshold," the amount of things in a space that we can safely handle without going over the edge. In the same way, a person with, let's say, a high gossip threshold, can afford to have a friend with a somewhat loose tongue, as most of his chatter will roll off and be ignored. Someone with a low threshold, however, is more likely to get caught up in the drama, and we can imagine that the two of them together might cause more trouble than either one alone. All persons are worthy of our respect; but they are not all good choices as close friends.

> Jenny Penny had... a round creamy face with a soft glossless cloud of soot-black hair about it and enormous dusky blue eyes with long tangled black lashes. When she slowly raised those lashes and looked at you with those scornful eyes you felt that you were a worm honoured in not being stepped on. You liked better to be snubbed by her than courted by any other: and to be selected as a temporary confidante of Jenny Penny's was an honour almost too great to be borne...

(L.M. Montgomery, *Anne of Ingleside*)

The blunt judgements of Discernment sometimes have to be toned down by **Appreciation**, who specializes in noticing "a trait of unselfishness here, of delicacy there, of honour elsewhere; to observe and treasure the record of the beauty of perfectness in any man's work, whether the work be a great poem or the sweeping of a room." But Sister Appreciation also has to deal with her own Daemons:

> Depreciation is the sneering Daemon who...may be inspired by the monster Envy, who is perpetually going about to put stumbling-blocks in the way of justice, and belittle the claims of others; or it may arise from Thoughtlessness, which is but a form of Self-occupation...We would not allow ourselves to depreciate if we recollected that Appreciation is one part of the Justice we owe to the characters and the

works of others. (pp. 148-149)

Veracity, Fidelity, Simplicity, and Sincerity must therefore direct our *words*. Candour, Appreciation, Discrimination must guide our *thoughts*. Fair-dealing, Honesty, Integrity must govern our *actions*. (p. 137, italics mine)

And they all serve under Mother Justice.

Scriptures to Ponder

But let judgment run down as waters, and righteousness as a mighty stream. (Amos 5:24)

Along the Way

Day 31: Truth is Not Violent

It's obvious that there is much overlap and cross-communication between the territories of our Self-Kingdom. For example, the question of what we say and how we say it begins in the physical realm, but it comes into its own through the work of Intellect, Imagination, and Reason; and is tempered in the House of Heart by Brothers Humility, Loyalty, and Gladness. We find that speech is also a frequent topic of conversation among the Sisters of Justice.

In their House, we are shown a large window (or lens) through which the happenings of the kingdom appear, framed as rights and duties. The sisters try to explain how it works.

Appreciation: For instance, Brother Sympathy might motivate you to speak to someone kindly, and so you do; but as we view it through this window, we see that a certain manner of words is *due* from us to those to whom we speak; and if we do not say these words, we are *unjust* to them. If we tell a lie about someone, that person has the *right* to be angry with us.

Candour: Yes, and when we are used to hearing untruths, we can be easily conditioned to *think untruly*, and then we find it hard even to see Sister Truth, or to hear her when other voices are loud. And that is a shame, because she is the most beautiful resident of the House of Heart (p. 153).

Discernment: There she is, walking behind Mother Justice. She is gentle and never violent, and is an important part of our House. But it rests with you to choose to hear her.

Candour: Be aware: those who step in front of her or who try to drown out her speech are often charming and well-mannered. If they were ugly or crude you might not be tempted to listen to them, but they are too clever for that. Beware of Suspicion, Treachery, and Calumny, or "Lady Slander" as we call her.

Appreciation: Watch out particularly for Envy, because she likes to twist things about and tell you that you are the one being treated unfairly. If someone dances better than you, you decide that you are not interested in dancing, that it is a waste of time. If someone dresses better than you, it must be because they waste too much time and money on themselves.

Candour: And if they speak better, Envy calls it "affectation." But you see, in this we deceive ourselves, and Truth is silenced.

Mother Justice and Truth enter, and everyone is quiet as they begin to speak.

Mother Justice: Most persons are careful to cherish Truth in all they say about the people in their own homes, but how many of us are equally careful in speaking of people who live next door? We may believe that we have a right to be critical, or simply that we are speaking the Truth; but if we use Truth to wound, Truth herself suffers.

Truth: I am here to serve Justice, but I must not be used as a weapon. Remember to use the glasses that Sister Candour has given you, so that you can see more than one side of a question, and understand that there are often brave and caring and good people, even among your opponents.

Mother Justice: Therefore we are courteous to the words of others; we listen, we do not contradict, we try to understand.

Truth: And when other persons express their opinions, however much they may differ from those in which we have been brought up, we keep ourselves from violence in thought and word, and listen with deference where we cannot agree. (p. 143)

Mother Justice: Francis Bacon said that "the belief of truth, which is the enjoying of it; is the sovereign good of human nature." Let us always cherish our dear Sister Truth.

Scriptures to Ponder

> ...If ye continue in my word, then are ye my
> disciples indeed; And ye shall know the truth, and
> the truth shall make you free. (John 8:31-32)

> Rejoice in the truth. (1 Cor. 13:6)

Along the Way

Day 32: Speaking the Truth in Love

Does the call to peace and gentleness in the last passage rule out speaking the truth boldly? We have many examples in Scripture of those who were called to speak before kings, judges, and religious leaders, often risking their own safety by saying things that those in authority did not want to hear.

How do we get to a place of speaking truth in love but also with boldness, Charlotte asks?

She was ahead of her time in this respect, especially concerning women's language patterns. She tells us to tell what we believe to be the fact, without adding qualifiers such as "At least I think so" or "Am I making sense?" We are to "be careful not to rush into statements without knowledge"; but habitually using expressions of uncertainty, implies just the opposite. Like false humility (see **Day 27**), it hinders more than it helps. That doesn't mean we need to stay out of conversations on subjects we know little about, but we can be honest about our limitations without pretending to know either a lot or nothing at all. And the second of those, according to Charlotte, can be just as annoying as the first.

Aim for "accurate observation and exact record." But as we have been shown, Sister Truth must be used with grace and courtesy. The sun will go on rising and setting even if someone else makes a mistake about what day it was or the man's name. We don't have to be fact cops for other people. Truth is also kind; she is cautious about treading on other people's sensitive spots, even to get a laugh.

Cultivate a useful vocabulary of alternative terms for words like love, hate, wonderful, stinks. Keep big, strong words for big, strong situations, so that after you've said that you love chocolate and raindrops and puppies, you won't be scratching your head to express what you feel about your friends, your parents, and God.

Where do Stories fit in?

Over the years that I homeschooled my children, I occasionally met people whose well-meant concern for Truth threw up a brick wall against all forms of fiction. One such person encouraged me to substitute books about "real" rabbits for Beatrix Potter's jacket-wearing, bread-and-milk-and-blackberry-eating Peter Rabbit. Charlotte differentiates between "accidental" and "essential" truth, or the "Truth of Art," but does not in any way devalue Peter.

> ... for example, given, such and such a character, he
> must needs have thought and acted in such and
> such a way, with such and such consequences...This
> sort of fiction is of enormous value to us, whether
> we find it in poetry or romance; it teaches us morals
> and manners; what to do in given circumstances;
> what will happen if we behave in a certain way...We
> cannot learn these things except through what is
> called fiction, or from the bitter experience of life,
> from the penalties of which our writers of fiction do
> their best to spare us. (p. 160)

Reading *Peter Rabbit* teaches us, more than any direct instruction could, why not to go into Mr. McGregor's garden. Also what "exert oneself" means, and that chamomile tea is good for calming down frantic young rabbits. These lessons are invaluable; and though their truth may be of the "artistic" sort, it is no less Truth.

Scriptures to Ponder

> But [that we] speaking the truth in love, may grow
> up into him in all things, which is the head, even
> Christ... (Ephesians 4:15)

Along the Way

Day 33: It Will Prevail (A Bit?)

In the chapter "Some Causes of Lying," Charlotte uses a military metaphor, describing Truth as a fortress under attack. In this battle,

> ...scrupulosity, rash generalisation, exaggeration,
> [and] amusing representation, are, as it were, the
> light skirmishers which assault [the] defences [of
> Truth] as chance offers; but there are also the
> sappers and miners who dig under its foundations...
> [such as] Malice and Envy, which lead to
> Calumny...(p. 163)

But let us take courage:

> Truth may be driven away, but she is there; and we
> must keep still hearts to hear her words and
> obedient tongues to speak them. (p. 152)

And Sister Truth has loyal assistants in her work for Justice:

> ...Veracity; Simplicity, whose part it is to secure that
> every spoken word means just what it appears to
> mean, and nothing more and nothing less:
> Sincerity, which secures that word of mouth tallies
> exactly with thought of heart, that we say exactly
> what we think: [and] Fidelity, which makes us

faithful to every promise at any cost—always
excepting such promises as should never have been
made; the only honourable thing that we can do is
to break a promise which is wrong in itself. (pp.
165-166)

Magna est Veritas

Charlotte ends the chapter with a Latin phrase: *Magna est Veritas et
Prævalebit.*

Now, there's a bit of humor connected with this, although it comes
after Charlotte's time. The phrase comes from the first Book of Esdras
in the Latin Vulgate Bible. Actually it should be *Magna est veritas et
prævalet,* "Great is truth and it prevails," but the last word is often
misquoted (as Charlotte did) as *prævalebit,* "will prevail." No great
damage there. British readers over a certain age, though, may have read
Billy Bunter's Bolt (1957), about a schoolboy who, among other things,
wasn't very good at Latin:

> 'You are the most untruthful boy in my form,
> Bunter. You must learn better, Bunter. You will
> write out, five hundred times, the sentence: *Magna
> est veritas, et praevalebit.* You know what that
> means, Bunter?'
>
> 'Oh! Yes, sir. It—it means, great is truth, and it will
> prevail a bit—.'

And somehow that joke stuck, because there was a bit of—er—truth in
it.

What is Truth?

As we approach the end of Lent, the word "truth" may also bring to
mind a darker moment from John 18:38: "Pilate saith unto him, What
is truth?" Did Jesus wonder, at that moment, if Truth would prevail—
even a bit?

To go back to Charlotte's era, an English poet named Coventry
Patmore (1823-1896) wrote a poem called "Magna est Veritas," which
ends like this:

When all its work is done, the lie shall rot;
The truth is great, and shall prevail,
When none cares whether it prevail or not.

Which is, perhaps, a good response. But we are still called to be among those who do care.

Scriptures to Ponder

Buy the truth, and sell it not; also wisdom, and
instruction, and understanding. (Proverbs 23:23)

And ye shall be hated of all men for my name's sake:
but he that endureth to the end shall be saved.
(Matt. 10:22)

Along the Way

Day 34: Do and Due (Justice in Action)

Looking through the Justice window, we see particular tasks in our day labelled "Must Be Done," and others as "May Be Done," "Can Wait Without Harm," or "Not So Important." "Must" is the word that resonates for Justice and her crew, and here we can use the help of Sister Discernment, but also her colleague Integrity. Sister Integrity is a hard worker, but she is also one of the most fun residents of the House of Justice. She allows each job the time that belongs to it, and never has to stress about things hanging over her head that should have been done last week, so she is always up for a swim or a game of ball when the work day is over.

...let us do each bit of work as perfectly as we know
how, remembering that each thing we turn out is a
bit of ourselves, and we must leave it whole and
complete; for this is Integrity. (p. 172)

During our visit to the House of Justice, three cheerful characters appear, asking for a night's lodging in exchange for some work; they answer to the names Idle, Careless, and Volatile. They keep everyone amused during the evening with all kinds of magic tricks and parlour games. They also claim to be great carpenters, so Sister Integrity promises to employ them in the morning, building a new chicken coop. The three of them show up bright and early to eat breakfast, and carry a mess of tools out back; but, two hours later when the Sisters come to inspect, the "carpenters" have parked themselves on a pile of wood, are drinking something from bottles and making music with a banjo and a wash-tub bass. And very little seems to have been built. Careless waves, and Volatile asks "When's lunch?" Sister Integrity, good-tempered as she usually is, is obviously put out, and that's what she does: puts them out.

As they leave through the back gate, grumbling and protesting, there's a knocking at the front. The Porter brings in three new travellers named Diligence, Attention and Perseverance, who are also wearing toolbelts and workboots. We wonder if there will be a repeat of last night's performance; but no, these three seem to be known by the Justice Sisters, and capable of finishing the job that the others abandoned. Do they want lunch first? No, they say they've just come to work, and so they do, with amazing results. The chicken house is completed in an hour, and they also fix a hole in the fence, mend a leaking tap, and change the furnace filter. Only then do they stop and have a quick snack, along with some prayer and worship with the Sisters. Sister Candour plays a guitar, and she's really quite good; when asked, she says that she took lessons from Imagination, but that Diligence and Perseverance helped her a great deal as well.

> It is astonishing how much time there is in a day, and how many things we can get in if we have a mind. It is also astonishing how a day, a week, or a year may slip through our fingers, and nothing done. (p. 173)

> We know [we need Perseverance] well enough as it applies to skating, hockey, and the like. We say we want practice, or, are out of practice, and must get some practice; but we do not realise that, in all the affairs of our life, the same thing holds good. What we have practice in doing we can do with ease, while

we bungle over that in which we have little practice.
(p. 208)

Why Worry?

But it's not just about the practical side of not letting your house be blown down, or the cost to the taxpayers when graffiti has to be scrubbed off or painted over, or the inconvenience to your friend when you borrow a book and forget to give it back. It's the chipping away at our character, the little unrepaired cracks and leaks, that Charlotte worries about.

> We may be guilty of many lapses which no one
> notices, but every lapse makes an imperfection in
> our own character...the habit of permitting
> ourselves in small dishonesties, whether in the way
> of waste of time, slipshod work, or injured property,
> prepares the way for a ruinous downfall in afterlife.
> But we need fear no fall, for Integrity is, with us, a
> part of 'ourselves,' and only asks of us a hearing. (p.
> 178)

Did you catch that last bit? We don't have to go searching far to find Integrity: she's already there in our spiritual DNA, just waiting to be encouraged.

> ...each thing we turn out [or use well] is a bit of
> ourselves, and we must leave it whole and complete;
> for this is Integrity. (p. 172)

Scriptures to Ponder

> Therefore, my beloved brethren, be ye stedfast,
> unmoveable, always abounding in the work of the
> Lord, forasmuch as ye know that your labour is not
> in vain in the Lord. (1 Cor. 15:58)

Along the Way

Loud Hosannas (Palm Sunday)

At first it seems pretty obvious that what we do fits into Justice; in fact, figuring out just (or unjust) action should be even easier than speech or thought. As we teach young children right from wrong, we usually focus first on physical obedience, on the things that they may or may not *do*. Right? But there is a need for Integrity in *how* things are done, that may elude many of us, even as adults; or, to put it another way, we may understand points of Justice in matters of Ten-Commandments-type morality, but not see the connection with our everyday activities. We don't steal, but we do borrow things from other people and forget to give them back (not out of malice, but possibly out of disorganization). We don't bear false witness, but we don't meet a deadline on a project, or make a needed phone call, because we let other less important tasks carry the day away.

> But to find [the next thing to do] is not, after all, so
> simple. It is often a matter of selection. There are
> twenty letters to write, a dozen commissions to do,
> a score of books you want to read, and much
> ordering and arranging of shelves and drawers that
> you would like to plunge into at once. (p.171)

If we are responsible for the training of children, we must teach them to take the trouble to do things well, even when no-one is watching (and that is so much better than making them behave by assigning toy elves to spy on them). We teach them not to dawdle, or to try to get other people to do their chores for them by "forgetting" or by doing the job so poorly that their parents give up and do it themselves, or even by waiting until somebody "makes" them do it. They learn that "makes" has to come first from the habits they are building, and then from Will. All this builds on itself as they grow up.

> Power comes by *doing* and not by *resolving*, and it
> is habit that serves us, whether it be the habit of
> Latin verse or of carving. Also, and this is a
> delightful thing to remember, every time we do a
> thing helps to form the habit of doing it; and to do a
> thing a hundred times without missing a chance,
> makes the rest easy. (pp. 208-209, italics hers)

A Hymn Story

You probably know this Palm Sunday hymn

> Hosanna, loud hosanna,
>
> The little children sang;
>
> Through pillared court and temple
>
> The lovely anthem rang.
>
> To Jesus, who had blessed them
>
> Close folded to His breast,
>
> The children sang their praises,
>
> The simplest and the best.

But did you know that the author, Jeanette Threlfall had a lifetime full of various types of suffering? She lost her parents at an early age, was always in poor health, and later was in a carriage accident in her fifties which caused her to be bedridden. She died only a few years after that, and Arthur Penrhyn Stanley, the Dean of Westminster, spoke at her funeral. This is what he said:

> ... when [life] has been changed from the enjoyment
> of everything to the enjoyment of nothing; when
> year by year, and week by week, the suffering, the
> weakness, have increased; and when yet, in spite of
> this, the patient sufferer has become the centre of
> the household, the adviser and counsellor of each;
> when there has been a constant stream of
> cheerfulness under the severest pain; when there
> has been a flow of gratitude for any act of kindness,
> however slight; when we recall the eager hope of
> such an one, that progress and improvement, not
> stagnation or repose, will be the destiny of the
> newly-awakened soul; then, when the end has
> come, we feel more than ever that the future is
> greater than the present.

The way we live our lives is often, indeed, a matter of selection.

Scriptures to Ponder

> And a very great multitude spread their garments in
> the way; others cut down branches from the trees,
> and strawed them in the way. And the multitudes
> that went before, and that followed, cried, saying,
> Hosanna to the son of David: Blessed is he that
> cometh in the name of the Lord; Hosanna in the
> highest. (Matthew 21:8-9)

Along the Way

Day 35: Justice in Thought

Justice in the Books We Read

A book which some homeschoolers have read is *Evaluating Books: What Would Thomas Jefferson Think About This?* Of course Thomas Jefferson's opinion on books is not the only one that matters to us; we might just as well ask what Albert Einstein or Jane Austen or any famous clergyperson might have thought. In the House of Justice, we have another tool available to us, the large window which shows us the Kingdom. As we use it to view the books in our own library, we notice that the parts of the glass opening on the reading tables are very thick, slightly scuffed, and hard to see through. "This glass does not make for easy reading," we complain, as we rub at the window.

Sister Discernment responds, "As a fact, the books which make us think, the poems which we ponder, the lives of men which we consider, are of more use to us than volumes of good counsel."

Sister Appreciation agrees, "We read 'good books,' thinking how good they are, and how good we are to read them! Then, whoosh, it all goes out of our minds, because the writer has put what he had to say so plainly that we have not had to think for ourselves."

Sister Integrity says, "It seems to be a law in the things of life and mind that we do not get anything for our own unless we work for it. That may be why the Lord told people stories which they might allow to pass lightly through their minds as an interest of the moment, or which they might think upon, form opinions upon, and find in them a guide to the meaning of their lives."

"But what if we can't see through the glass properly, and we get the wrong ideas?" we ask.

"Well, of course you will," says Sister Candour. "Your opinions about books and other things will very likely be wrong, and you will yourself correct them by and by when you have read more, thought more, know more." (pp. 183-184, adapted)

The Value of Opinions

As we walk in the garden with Mother Justice, she reminds us to keep on the paths, even within the walls of the House: off to one side, there is poison ivy mixed with the other plants. "We've heard the saying 'leaves of three, let it be,'" we say. "But aren't there good plants also with three leaves? How can we tell the difference?"

"You're right about that," she says. "And poison ivy doesn't always have shiny leaves, as we are sometimes told." She shows us (without getting too close) things that do give it away: the leaflets alternate along the stem; the middle leaflet of the three tends to have a longer stem than the two side leaflets; and, often, one side of the leaflet will have "teeth," or appear jagged, while the other is round and smooth.

"And of course," she says, "you can know poison ivy by its fruits: white berries early in the year, and red later on. Do you know one way that poison ivy gets spread? Animals and birds eat the berries, but they don't digest the seeds, so…well, that's one way new plants get started. But as for helpful plants that have three leaves, yes, and there are some that even look much like poison ivy: Boston Ivy, Virginia Creeper. And Box Elder, *Acer negundo*. Its wood has many uses; it can be carved and turned. The trees make good homes for wildlife. The Box Elder can even be tapped for its sap."

"But if you can't avoid having poison ivy in the abbey grounds," we muse, "why not keep from growing the lookalike plants? Then there would be no confusion."

Mother Justice breaks off some Box Elder leaves and hands them to us.

"Three leaves," she says, "from a plant that is worth preserving. And three rules, then, as to an opinion that is worth the having. First, we must have thought about the subject and know something about it. When we want an opinion about the weather that is worth having, we consult the gardener, or a farmer, or sailor, for the business of these men has made them observant of weather signs.

"Second, it must be our own opinion, and not caught up by chance remarks. Lastly, it must not be influenced by our inclination, or subject to our whims. Why have Box Elder at all? Because it is a useful and beautiful plant, even if it can be confused with one that causes trouble. Why have opinions at all? Because they are a needed part of our life. The person who thinks out his opinions modestly and carefully is doing his duty as truly as if he helped to save a life. There is no 'more or less' about duty; and it is a great part of our work in life to do our duty in our thoughts and form just opinions." (pp. 179-181)

Sister Truth, who has been quietly following along, adds this: "As you know, we have a mentor within us, about which I shall have to speak more fully later; but, once we get into the habit of bringing our thoughts before Conscience, we shall soon be able to distinguish as to the right or wrong of an opinion before we utter it." (p. 181)

Scriptures to Ponder

> And in the morning, It will be foul weather to day: for the sky is red and lowring. O ye hypocrites, ye can discern the face of the sky; but can ye not discern the signs of the times? (Matthew 16:3)

Along the Way

Day 36: Arriving at an Opinion

In Which We Are Sent Off Again

The Sisters agree that it is time for us to discover Opinion for ourselves, a place located several miles down the road. They kindly fill our packs with supplies, and give us some parting advice.

Discernment: 'Read, mark, learn, and inwardly digest'; listen and consider, being sure that one of the purposes you are in the world for is, to form right opinions about all matters that come in your way.

Appreciation: But avoid the short road to Opinion.

Truth: Don't be sidetracked by Fallacy.

Us: How will we know when we have arrived there?

Candour: Indeed, you may not be entirely sure, and, in fact, someone else may tell you that you have not yet arrived there; but because it is your thinking, in fact your very own property that will come to you through pondering, you must hold to it firmly.

Discernment: You will always have Mother Justice at hand to help you claim your Opinion. But do not be sluggish about getting there, or hesitant to knock on the door.

Us: Why?

Appreciation: If you fail to take hold of it, it may disappear before your eyes! (pp. 185-186, adapted)

We decide that we had better lose no time in setting out.

Staking our Claim

How is it, we wonder, that we can lay claim to this out-of-the-way place called Opinion? We are told that it is built on Principles, which may have been laid down by ourselves, or inherited from someone else, but in either case we make them our own because we act on them.

> These opinions rule our conduct, and they are called
> Principles because they are *princeps*, first or chief
> in importance of all the opinions we hold...*everyone*
> has principles—that is, *everyone* has a few chief and
> leading opinions upon which every bit of his
> conduct is based. (p. 187, italics mine)

Those principles are not always obvious when we first view our Opinion; but if we go around the back and do some fishing in the creek, they are bound to come up. For example, a lazy worker might be operating on these principles:

> 'What's the good of doing more than you can help?'
> 'What's the good of hurrying a fellow? I'm not going
> to hustle!' (p. 187)

It's not that he doesn't have principles, just that he has poor ones.

> Another fellow is punctual, prompt, and diligent in
> his work; he hardly knows why himself, but he has
> gathered, by degrees, certain principles upon which
> he cannot help acting. He remembers that he owes
> it to his parents and teachers to work; that what he
> *owes*, he *ought* to do; it is his duty...He may have
> heard such things as these said at home or at
> school, or they may have come into his head, he
> does not know how; but, anyway, he has taken them
> for his chief things, *his principles*, and he acts upon
> them always. (p. 188, italics hers)

When Loyalty Meets Principles

But as we see when we finally do arrive at Opinion, potential principles are not only to be found in the creek, but they come at us from all directions. Various people are shouting at us from the windows and the porch. The outer walls are covered with posters telling us to vote for this, buy that, read this, try these. All kinds of things can come up on our fishing lines, and many ideas compete for our attention. As Charlotte says, making sense of it all can be clamorous and tiresome (p. 188); the problem is choosing which ones to keep and which to throw back; which ones we will finally claim for our own. How do we discriminate between them?

> ...by and by, as character develops, convictions grow
> upon us which come to be bound up with our being.
> These, not catchwords caught up here and there
> from the newspapers or from common talk, are our
> principles—possessions that we have worked out

86

with labour of thought and, perhaps, pain of feeling.
He is true to himself who is true to these; and no
other. (p. 124)

We gather our principles unconsciously; but they
are our masters; and it is our business every now
and then to catch one of them, look it in the face,
and question ourselves as to the manner of conduct
such a principle must bring forth. (p. 190)

Being able to catalogue all our principles isn't always necessary. But it
is a good idea, every now and then, to dip a line in the water and take
a look at them.

[Our true] principles are always written in
characters of their own. (p. 189)

In other words, you can see someone's principles in his face, and they
can make us either trust him or think we should be cautious. However,
this takes practice, and can be distorted by our prejudices; and some
of us are just better at it than others.

'Strewth!' the Superintendent had said. 'One chance
out of twelve, and you made it. That was good
going. He picked your man out of the bunch,' he
said in explanation to the local Inspector.

'Did you know him?' the Inspector said, a little
surprised. 'He's never been in trouble before, as far
as we know.'

'No, I never saw him before. I don't even know what
the charge is.'

'Then what made you pick him?'

Grant had hesitated, analysing for the first time his
process of selection...At last, having delved into his
subconscious, he blurted: 'He was the only one of
the twelve with no lines on his face.'

(Josephine Tey, *The Daughter of Time*)

Scriptures to Ponder

Through wisdom is an house builded; and by

understanding it is established: And by knowledge shall the chambers be filled with all precious and pleasant riches. (Proverbs 24:3-4)

Along the Way

Day 37: Downhill All the Way

A note on this chapter: The language Charlotte uses to describe addictions and also body shape and size may be offensive (or at least excessive) to current-day ears. Please give her some grace here, understanding that she is attempting to show the need to moderate our appetites and desires (of all kinds), and to submit these things as well to the management of our Heavenly Father.

Oh My...

We lay claim to our place of Opinion, but realize that our journey through the kingdom is not quite finished. Where to go next? We decide to follow the creek, jotting things in our nature notebooks (and not forgetting to watch for birds in the branches, see **Day 11**). Eventually the creek crosses with a footpath, and we see a sign-post pointing in one direction, that says "No-Harm." However, we look in the guidebook that Mother Justice slipped into our lunch basket, and read this warning:

> Now, 'No-Harm' is a dangerous sign-post to follow. It points to a broad road [where] the going is easy, because it is downhill all the way. This is the road of self-indulgence; and whenever we have to justify anything we do to ourselves by saying, 'There's no harm in it,' we may be pretty sure we are on the downward grade. Our only chance then is to struggle back by the uphill track of duty. (p. 194)

The book goes on:

> [The one] choosing to go the way that gives him no trouble, comes by and by to a parting of the ways; to

> the four cross-roads. [The first one is called
> Drunkenness]; the other byways branching off the
> Broad Road lead to the quarters of Gluttony, Sloth,
> and Unchastity...Some persons hover between the
> four cross-roads, now going down one, now
> another, and now another; but others—like the
> drunkard, the gourmand, the slothful person, and
> the unclean—choose their way and stick to it, letting
> themselves be lost, body and soul, in the pursuit of
> some lust of the body. (pp. 194-198)

Going down No-Harm Road doesn't sound at all like a good idea, and, honestly, we're a little bit shocked that these places still exist in the kingdom. Drunkenness? Gluttony? Sloth? Unchastity? How is it that we're back to these how-low-can-you-go House of Body issues? Maybe that's part of it, that we think we're better than all that. We've got a motivated House of Heart and a functioning Intellect, a Soul in pretty good repair, so we'd probably be okay with just a little stroll to the crossroads, maybe a short walk down one sideroad or another. Yes?

Why does this fall under the heading of "Justice to Ourselves?" Because, first and most literally, excesses do harm our bodies and minds. But it's also a form of ingratitude, like a child carelessly breaking the toy he's just been given.

> Is this a just return to God for the wonderful
> endowments of body and mind this man has
> received? Is it just to his family and neighbours to
> make himself a burden and an offence? Is it just to
> himself—that wonderful, beautiful self, with all its
> powers of heart, mind and soul, of which it is
> everyone's first business to make the most? (p. 196)

Second, if you don't keep your body "in temperance, soberness, and chastity," as Charlotte quotes her church's catechism, you not only injure yourself, but you can become a bad neighbour to other people, both by the things you do or don't do, and by your negative influence on them. Which isn't loving your neighbour, is it?

No More Pie

A Scottish helper on a western ranch was invited to

dinner by his employer. He ate a large piece of apple pie with such relish that his hostess offered him a second helping. "No more, thank you kindly, ma'am," he replied. "I would na wish to become an addict." (N. B. Miller, included in *Fun Fare: A Reader's Digest Treasury of Wit and Humor*)

Is temperance important simply because if you eat too many pieces of pie you'll get cavities, or put on weight, or because that overindulgence might lead someone else astray? Or because you don't want to appear greedy? No, there's a bigger reason why too much is a problem. "It means that the person who indulges in excesses has lost control over himself, so that there is some one thing he *must* have or *must* do, at whatever loss to himself or inconvenience to others." (p. 192)

This is why Charlotte calls temperance "self-ordering." It comes down to her core principle of living objectively, with will, not willfulness; with choice, not by whim or by the suggestions (even well-reasoned) of others, if those suggestions lure us out of our path (or our calling). And don't forget that we are not thrown only to our own willpower, but that we are promised an abundant supply of help.

Scriptures to Ponder

Watch and pray, that ye enter not into temptation: the spirit indeed is willing, but the flesh is weak. (Matthew 26:41)

That we henceforth be no more children, tossed to and fro... (Ephesians 4:14)

Along the Way

Day 38: The Upper Chambers (Maundy Thursday)

...Love and Justice are inseparable from Mansoul; they are there, and we must take count of them. Not that they are as self-adjusting wheels, so to speak, which go right whether we will or no. On the

> contrary, [they] require the continual supervision of
> the Prime Minister, himself ruled by the higher
> Power; and without such over-looking they produce
> tangles in the lives of men. (p. 136)

> We may believe that the Creator is honoured by our
> attempt to know something of the powers and the
> perils belonging to that human nature with which
> He has endowed us. (*Book II*, p. 4)

While some studies of this book may focus almost exclusively on the government offices, this time we have gone to the edges of Mansoul, and had a glimpse of places beyond. We have almost completed the journey, and yet it seems that we have barely spoken of some of the most powerful characters in the kingdom. *Book I*, being aimed at the younger Selves, speaks much more of the interdependence of heart, mind, and body than it does of Will and Conscience, leaving these subjects, like the study of actual government, for the upper years. And we have hardly even spoken of the House of the Soul, the final "division" of the Kingdom, although (as Charlotte says early on) there really is no division.

Near the end of the chapter "Self-Ordering: Justice to Ourselves," Charlotte inserts a little teaser for *Book II*. Perhaps, she says, we have gone down one of the four Roads to Ruin, by allowing unclean thoughts to enter our minds. In words that evoke our own time, she admits that "we cannot help coming across what may lead to evil imaginings."

> ...[But] perhaps if we could there would be no battle
> to fight, and then we could not obey the command,
> "Glorify God with your bodies." Every one of us
> must get the power to draw down the blinds, as it
> were, not to let imagination picture the unclean
> thing...look at the thoughts you let in, and shut the
> door upon intruders. (pp. 202-203)

When we get to the point that we see the need to learn to draw down the blinds—and to understand the power within us to do so—then it is the right time to begin to learn about how the Conscience must be instructed, and that the Will must be given extensive, though sometimes difficult and uncomfortable, authority in the kingdom.

From the mere greed of eating and drinking to
ambition, that 'last infirmity of noble minds,' every
single power of Mansoul will, if it be permitted,
make for misrule. But, courage, my Lord Will! and
the forces fall into place and obey the word of
command. (*Book II*, p. 141)

Like the Prime Minister serving a king, though, the Will is not left
entirely on his own, even in these early days.

Pray every day and every night with the confidence
of a child speaking to his father,— "Our Father
which art in Heaven, lead us not into temptation";
and then, think no more of the matter, but live all
you can the beautiful, full life of body and mind,
heart and soul, for which our Father has made
provision. (p. 203)

Scriptures to Ponder

And I will pray the Father, and he shall give you
another Comforter, that he may abide with you for
ever; Even the Spirit of truth; whom the world
cannot receive, because it seeth him not, neither
knoweth him: but ye know him; for he dwelleth
with you, and shall be in you. (John 14:16-17)

Along the Way

Day 39: Offering Ourselves (Good Friday)

The people also wondered much to behold him only,
seeing always such a number of labourers, artificers,
ambassadors, officers, soldiers, and learned men,
whom he easily satisfied and dispatched...Thus he
won the good will of the common people, being
more popular and familiar in his conversation and
deeds, than he was otherwise in his orations. But the

greatest pains and care he took upon him was in
seeing the highways mended, the which he would
have as well done, as profitably done. (Plutarch, *Life
of Gaius Gracchus*)

I Will Make You...

In the final chapter of *Book I*, "Vocation," Charlotte describes a child's
heart that "reaches out wistfully" for "chances of usefulness," for
"world-work upon some task that is wanted." But the school
valedictorian or sports captain may be less successful after graduation,
"because the person with these attractive qualities may be like a vessel
without ballast, at the mercy of winds and waves." (p. 205) Or like a
chicken coop built by Idle, Careless, and Volatile.

> Everyone has immense 'chances,' as they are called;
> but the business of each is to be ready for his
> chance. The boy who got a medal from the Royal
> Humane Society for saving life, was ready for his
> chance; he had learned to swim; and, also, he had
> practised himself in the alert mind and generous
> temper which made him see the right thing to do
> and do it on the instant, without thought of the
> labour or danger of his action; without any thought,
> indeed, but of the struggling, sinking creature in the
> water. (pp. 205-206)

Learning to swim may be exactly what God wants of us. But this skill
in itself is of no more value than accounting, truck-driving, or speaking
Spanish, if it does not also lead us to see clearly and act generously,
with every power of Mind and Heart at our disposal.

> It is such persons as these the world wants, persons
> who have worked over every acre of that vast estate
> of theirs which we have called Mansoul; men and
> women ordered in nerve and trained in muscle, self-
> controlled and capable; with well-stored
> imagination, well-practised reason; loving, just, and
> true. (p. 206)

Fishers of Men

People through the centuries have wondered what sort of child Jesus might have been, if he was without sin: would that have made him an unpopular prig, focused only on his own goodness? Knowing what we do of his adult interactions with others, that wouldn't seem to be the case. It seems more likely that he might have been the sort of family anchor that Charlotte describes here:

> In most families there is the brother who cuts
> whistles and makes paper boats for the little ones,
> who gallops like a war-horse with Billy on his back,
> whom his mother trusts with messages and his
> father with commissions of importance; or, there is
> the sister to whose skirts the babies cling, who has
> learnt Latin enough to help her young brothers in
> their tasks...who writes notes for her mother and
> helps to nurse the baby through measles. (p. 207)

If those sorts of things (in a first-century Nazareth version) were indeed part of Jesus' early life, we might wonder if they came back to his mind during the years that he taught his disciples; the times that he healed the sick, rowed out with fishermen, welcomed children; and the days when the darkness seemed to be closing in, and he began to see fully what was required. Did his mind ever go back to toy boats and piggyback rides, chores in the carpenter shop or the kitchen, helping with a Hebrew lesson, caring for frail grandparents or under-the-weather siblings? Were there afternoons when Jesus had free time and, as he said later to Peter, "walkedst whither [he] wouldest?" In the same conversation, he foresaw Peter's later life:

> ...thou shalt stretch forth thy hands, and another
> shall gird thee, and carry thee whither thou
> wouldest not...And when he had spoken this, he
> saith unto him, Follow me. (John 21:18-19)

Maybe we're young, maybe we're old. Maybe we have a lot of personal freedom and choices; maybe we have skills; maybe people recognize our capabilities. Or maybe not. Maybe somebody or something else, sympathetic or not, seems to be controlling our circumstances right now. But there is still only one requirement. To follow.

Scriptures to Ponder

> Greater love hath no man than this, that a man lay
> down his life for his friends. (John 15:13)

Along the Way

Day 40: Pilgrim's Inn (Holy Saturday)

In a Cistercian monastery, in medieval times, the Porter would be on duty all day long at the gate, acting as the cheerful face of the abbey to the outside world. He greeted visitors and made their arrival known; but he had another special job: distributing food and clothing to poor people in the area. At Beaulieu Abbey in Hampshire, England, the Porter was responsible for choosing thirteen needy people every night to be fed and sheltered in the abbey's hospice (the place where travellers and pilgrims could sleep).

But there was one part of the monastic life in which the Porter could not fully participate. Unless he had a helper, he could not leave his post while the Offices were being sung, so instead he would pull up his hood and remain silently in his place until the prayers were done.

Imagine that the House of Love belongs to the Cistercian order, and that, on a sunny and hot afternoon, you arrive at the gate. Perhaps you have come a long way and are hoping for a room for the night. Your food basket is empty, and the extra clothes you packed are worn out. Unfortunately, the bell has just rung for the afternoon office, so you will have to wait until the Porter pulls down his hood and is able to talk to you.

So you sit on a low wall in the garden and think about where you have been. You listen to the monks chanting and the birds singing. You watch the bees on the flowers. You pray for the well-being of those you love. You realize that, while you may think you are at one of the Houses of Heart, this place has taken on the aspect of the House of Soul:

> ... the name we give to that within us which has

capacity for the knowledge and love of God, for
prayer and praise and faith, for the enthronement of
the King, whose right it is to reign over Mansoul.
(*Book II*, p. 4)

And, our search and demand for goodness and
beauty baffled here, disappointed there—it is only in
our God we find the whole. (*Book II*, p. 176)

You begin to hum an almost-forgotten hymn:

Open now thy gates of beauty,
Zion, let me enter there,
Where my soul in joyful duty
Waits for Him who answers prayer.
Oh, how blessed is this place,
Filled with solace, light and grace!

(German words by Benjamin Schmolk, translated
by Catherine Winkworth)

And you realize that having to wait can sometimes be the greatest
blessing of all.

Scriptures to Ponder

Joseph of Arimathaea, an honourable counseller,
which also waited for the kingdom of God, came,
and went in boldly unto Pilate, and craved the body
of Jesus. (Mark 15:43)

And not only they, but ourselves also, which have
the firstfruits of the Spirit, even we ourselves groan
within ourselves, waiting for the adoption, to wit,
the redemption of our body. For we are saved by
hope: but hope that is seen is not hope: for what a
man seeth, why doth he yet hope for? But if we hope
for that we see not, then do we with patience wait
for it. (Romans 8:23-25)

Along the Way

Three Magic Pearls (Resurrection Sunday)

What a treasure I have
In this wonderful peace,
Buried deep in the heart of my soul,
So secure that no power
Can mine it away,
While the years of eternity roll!

(Warren D. Cornell, "Wonderful Peace")

Frederick Buechner wrote in more than one place about his fondness for of L. Frank Baum's *Oz* books, particularly *Rinkitink in Oz*:

> [Rinkitink] and his young friend Prince Inga of
> Pingaree came into possession of three magic
> pearls—a blue one that conferred such strength that
> no power could resist it; a pink one that protected
> its owner from all dangers; and a pure white one
> that could speak words of great wisdom and
> helpfulness. (Buechner, *The Sacred Journey*)

Like *Rinkitink in Oz*, Charlotte's story of *Ourselves* also contains pearls that we can draw on for strength, protection, and wisdom.

The Pearl of Strength

> All sense of bondage ceases when we say, "I rejoice
> to do thy will, O my God; yea, thy law is within my
> heart." And, with this spring of glad obedience
> within us, we arise and shine, because every feeble,
> faltering step is sustained; when we fall we are
> raised, when we pause we are strengthened and
> cheered to go on; and, poor things as we know
> ourselves to be, our path is that of the just, shining
> more and more unto the perfect day. (*Book II*, p.
> 124)

The Pearl of Protection

Whenever life becomes so strenuous that we are off guard, then is our hour of danger. Ideas that make for vanity, petulance, or what not, assault us, and our safety lies in an ejaculation of prayer,— 'O God, make speed to save us! O Lord, make haste to help us!' and then, quick as thought, we must turn our eyes away from the aggravating circumstance and think of something diverting or interesting. (*Book II*, p. 168)

The Pearl of Wisdom

It is difficult to find a name which covers what we are and what we may become, but let us call it philosophy; for to know ourselves is wisdom...Man is not for himself, and to get out of ourselves and into the wide current of human life, of all sorts and conditions, is our wisdom and should be our care. (*Book II*, pp. 106-107)

The Ending

Every fairy tale must have a happy ending, of course—a *eucatastrophe*, or sudden joyous 'turn,' as Tolkien calls it—and *Rinkitink* is no exception. [The villains] Cor and Gos get their just deserts. The captive peoples are set free from their cruel bondage, and 'with sobs and tears of joy,' as Baum describes it, King Kitticut and Queen Garee are reunited with the son who has saved them. (Buechner, "Rinkitink in Oz," in *The Longing for Home*)

And there is a joyous celebration, at which the characters from *Rinkitink* meet up with all the regulars from the other *Oz* books. So we imagine a similar banquet, at which we meet all those who serve, create, nourish and govern in Mansoul: Imagination with his camera, the

98

Connoisseur with his paintbox, and Sister Candour with her eyeglasses; busy Reason, cheerful Generosity, and quiet Truth. (The daemons, like Cor and Gos, are no longer a threat.) And at the head of the table is the One with whom we are forever reunited.

The Son Who Has Saved Them

The day of resurrection! Earth, tell it out abroad;
The Passover of gladness, the Passover of God.
From death to life eternal, from earth unto the sky,
Our Christ hath brought us over, with hymns of
victory...

Now let the heavens be joyful! Let earth the song
begin!
Let the round world keep triumph, and all that is
therein!
Let all things seen and unseen their notes in
gladness blend,
For Christ the Lord hath risen, our joy that hath no
end.

(Translated from Greek to English by John M.
Neale, 1862)

A Final Word

When Rinkitink ran away from his subjects because he decided that the duties of kingship were too confining, he took with him a parchment entitled *How to be Good.* (*The Longing for Home*)

"This scroll," said Rinkitink, "is indeed a masterpiece. Its advice is of tremendous value. 'Never step on another man's toes.'" (*Rinkitink in Oz*)

Bibliography

Baum L. F. (1916). *Rinkitink in Oz.* Chicago, IL: Reilly & Lee.

Berenbaum, D. (Writer), & Favreau, J. (Director). (2003). *Elf* [Motion picture]. United States: New Line Cinema (presents) Guy Walks into a Bar Productions.

Buckley, A. (1899). *The fairy-land of science.* London: Edward Stanford.

Buechner, F. (1991). *Now and then: A memoir of vocation.* San Francisco, CA: HarperSanFrancisco.

Buechner, F. (1996). *The longing for home: recollections and reflections.* San Francisco, CA: HarperSanFrancisco.

Buechner, F. (1982). *The sacred journey.* San Francisco, CA: HarperSanFrancisco.

Buechner, F. (1977). *Telling the truth.* New York, NY: Harper & Row.

Bunyan, J. (1678). *The pilgrim's progress.* (Also: *The holy war, 1672*)

Byatt, A. S. (2016). *Peacock & vine: Fortuny and Morris in life and at work.* London: Chatto & Windus, an imprint of Vintage.

Carroll L. (1872). *Through the looking-glass and what Alice found there.* London, England: Macmillan and Co.

Cholmondeley, E. (2021). *The story of Charlotte Mason, 1842-1923.* Bristol, England: Lutterworth Press.

Collins, M. (1992). *"Ordinary" children, extraordinary teachers.* Norfolk, VA: Hampton Roads Pub. Co.

Cook, R.J. (1929). *One hundred and one famous poems with a prose supplement.* Chicago, IL: The Cable Company. ("Invictus")

Coon, G.L.. (Writer), Roddenberry, G. (Writer), & Pevney, J.. (Director). (1967). The devil in the dark [Television series episode]. In G. Roddenberry (Creator) & G.L. Coon, J.M. Lucas, & F. Freiberger (Producers), *Star Trek: The Original Series*. Desilu Productions.

Davis, M. (1980). It's hard to be humble. On *It's Hard to be Humble* [LP]. Los Angeles, CA: Casablanca Record and FilmWorks.

Dickens, C. (1843). *A Christmas carol.*

Emmert, K.P. (2015, February 18). A Lent that's not for your spiritual improvement. *Christianity Today*. Retrieved from www.christianitytoday.com

Farjeon, E. (1956). *The little bookroom*. New York, NY: H.Z. Walck.

Fisher, D. C. (1917). *Understood Betsy*. New York, NY: Grosset & Dunlap.

Foster, R. J. (2005). *Freedom of simplicity*. San Francisco, CA: HarperSanFrancisco.

Frye, N. (1963). *The educated imagination*. Toronto, ON: Canadian Broadcasting Corporation.

Fulghum, R. (1990). *All I really need to know I learned in kindergarten: Uncommon thoughts on common things*. Grafton Books.

Goodrich, F.(Writer), Hackett, A. (Writer), & Capra, F. (Writer/Director). (1946). *It's a wonderful life* [Motion picture]. United States: Liberty Films.

Goudge, E. (1948). *The herb of grace*. London: Hodder & Stoughton. (U.S. title *Pilgrim's inn*)

Goudge, E. (1960) *The dean's watch*. London: Hodder & Stoughton.

Grahame, K. (1908). *The wind in the willows*.

Jeanette Threlfall [Wikipedia entry]. (n.d.). Retrieved January 14, 2023, from https://en.wikipedia.org/wiki/Jeanette_Threlfall

Karon, J. (2002). *In this mountain*. New York, NY: Viking.

Kingsley, C. (1986). *The water babies*. New York, Children's Classics.

Kirkpatrick, W.J. (1899). *Gospel praises for use in meetings of Christian worship*. Hall-Mack. ("Wonderful Peace")

Lewis, C. S. (2010). *The chronicles of Narnia*. New York, NY: Barnes & Noble, Inc.

Lewis, C. S. (2001). *The great divorce: a dream*. New York, NY: HarperCollins.

MacDonald, B.H. (1947). *Mrs. Piggle-Wiggle*. New York, NY: J.B. Lippincott.

Macfarlane, R. (2015). *Landmarks*. London: Hamish Hamilton.

Macfarlane, R. (2018). *The lost words: A spell book*. Toronto, ON: House of Anansi Press.

Mason, C. M. (1905/1989). *Ourselves*. Reprint, with foreword by by John Thorley. Wheaton, IL: Tyndale House.

(Unknown) (1969). *The Mennonite hymnal*. Scottdale, PA., and Newton, KS: Herald Press and Faith and Life Press.

Montgomery, L. M. (1989). *Anne of Ingleside*. Bantam Books.

Oliver, M. (2016). *Blue horses*. Penguin Books.

Plutarch & North, T. (trans.) (1894/5). *Lives of the noble Grecians and Romans*. London: Dent.

Quiller, Couch, A. (ed.) (1939). *The Oxford book of English verse, new edition.* The University Press, Oxford. ("Magna est Veritas")

Rambo, R. [or Reba] (2011). Because of whose I am. On *The Lady's Treasury* [CD].Nashville, TN: Rambo McGuire Music.

Reader's Digest Association. (1949). *Fun fare: A treasury of Reader's Digest wit and humor*

Richards F. (1957). *Billy Bunter's bolt.* London: Cassell.

Ruskin, J. (1907). *Sesame and lilies.* London: G. Routledge.

Schaeffer, E. (1975). *What is a family?* Old Tappan, NJ: F.H. Revell Col.

Teale, E.W. (1951). *North with the spring.* New York, NY: Dodd, Mead, & Co.

Tey, J. (2013). *The daughter of time.* New York, NY: Touchstone, a division of Simon & Schuster.

Van der Post, L., & Parry, L. (2003). *William Morris and Morris & Co.* London: V. & A. Publications; published in association with Arthur Sanderson & Sons Ltd.

White, A. (2020). *Honest, simple souls.*

White, D.K. (2018, April 16). One thing that's way over my clutter threshold. [Web log message]. Retrieved from https://www.aslobcomesclean.com/2018/04/one-thing-thats-way-over-my-clutter-threshold/

White, D.K. (2020, January 13). What's the point of daily habits in an overly cluttered home? [Web log message]. Retrieved from https://www.aslobcomesclean.com/2020/01/whats-the-point-of-daily-habits-in-an-overly-cluttered-home/

Made in the USA
Coppell, TX
27 February 2025

46486681R10066